VICTORIAN EMBROIDERY

VICTORIAN EMBROIDERY

FREDA PARKER

Photography by Di Lewis

CRESCENT BOOKS
New York

First published in Great Britain in 1990
by Anaya Publishers Ltd, Strode House,
44–50 Osnaburgh Street, London NW1 3ND

This 1991 edition published by Crescent Books,
distributed by Outlet Book Company, Inc., a Random House Company,
225 Park Avenue South, New York, New York 10003.

Frontispiece: 'The New Hat' by Edouard Mentha (1858–1915). Fine Art Photographic Library
Endpapers: 19th-century Kutch embroidery skirt piece, Bombay State.
Bridgeman Art Library/Victoria & Albert Museum

ISBN 0-517-06588-6

Editor: Eve Harlow
Designer: Bob Hook
Picture Researcher: Andrea Stern
Charts: John Hutchinson and Dennis Hawkins
Colour trace-offs: Margaret Leaman
Technique drawings: Coral Mula

8 7 6 5 4 3 2

Typeset by Chapterhouse, The Cloisters, Formby, Nr. Liverpool
Colour reproduction by Columbia Offset, Singapore
Printed and bound in Hong Kong

CONTENTS

Introduction 6

BEADWORK 10
Floral Footstool • Gothic Cushion • Jet-beaded Dress
Silken Beaded Purse

SAMPLERS 20
House and Garden Sampler • Alphabet Sampler
Flower and Bird Motifs

BERLIN WOOLWORK 30
Slippers • Chrysanthemum Cushion
Turkish-style Case • Golden Bee Box

SURFACE EMBROIDERY 40
Georgette Stole • Roses and Forget-me-nots • Velvet Cap
Floral Greetings • Handkerchief for a Lady • Flower Frame
Fruit and Flowers • Paisley Table Cloth

WHITEWORK 68
Ribbon-tied Christening Robe • Round-necked Christening
Robe • Mountmellick Cushion • Alphabet for Linens

RIBBONWORK 84
Flower Picture • Florentine

CREWELWORK 90
Pomegranate and Parrot

SMOCKING 96
Heart Motifs

PINCUSHIONS 100
A Collection of Pincushions

A VICTORIAN CHRISTMAS 104
Village House • A Christmas Stocking • Jewelled Ornaments

FINISHING TOUCHES 108
Fringes and Tassels

TECHNIQUES FOR PERFECTION 114

Index 126

Acknowledgements 128

INTRODUCTION

The home was the centre of Victorian life. This was particularly true of the growing middle classes, who liked to fill their houses with furniture and bric-à-brac in the comfortable, crowded style that was typical of the period. The Victorian home often also combined an exuberant mixture of styles, including Gothic, Renaissance, Elizabethan and Eastern.

Furniture was rounded and very thickly padded. Strong colours, that might be considered gaudy today, were widely used and many different patterns were put together. Windows were heavily draped with as many as three layers of fabric for curtains and blinds, and with a decorative pelmet above. Mantelpieces, shelves, tables and the piano were also draped. Pictures covered the walls and every available surface had its share of ornaments.

For the working classes sewing was, of course, a practical necessity. It was a skill needed to make and mend around the home and perhaps to supplement a meagre income. For the middle and upper classes sewing played a different, but equally prominent, role. Women from these classes had enough domestic help to give them plenty of time on their hands. Paid employment was unthinkable for ladies, and very few girls were given an academic education. However, the Victorian work ethic deplored idleness, and so young ladies kept themselves busy with such refined accomplishments as drawing, painting, music, singing, dancing, and, of course, needlework. Their sewing would include making and repairing household items and producing garments for the poor, but the greatest part of their time was spent on embroidery and fancy work.

Victorian ladies embroidered a wide variety of articles for the home including chair covers, firescreens, footstools, bell-pulls, table-covers, tie-backs and elaborate pelmets called lambrequins. Some personal items they worked – for example, album and prayerbook covers, pen wipers, blotters, watch pockets and cigar cases – are now obsolete. Numerous designs for embroidery were published in periodicals of the time.

It is widely imagined that Victorian ladies spent long hours patiently plying their needles to produce beautiful work with perfect, tiny stitches. In fact, as can be seen from some of the original examples in this book, this was not always the case. Some of them appear to have been produced more for quick effect.

The materials and fabrics used for embroidery in the Victorian period were varied, ranging from silk to leather. Even punched card was used to produce such things as counted thread pictures and bookmarks. Threads were of wool, cotton and silk in different types and weights. Silk was more readily available than it is now. Gold and silver threads were popular also as was ribbon. In addition, more eccentric materials such as straw, fish scales, feathers and beetles' wings were sometimes incorporated into the work.

Various types of embroidery are particularly associated with the Victorian period. Best among them is perhaps the white embroidery on white fabric known as whitework. This included the delicate Ayrshire work, stitched on very fine cotton, which was a technique imported to Scotland from France early in the nineteenth century. In the late 1800s a much heavier type of white embroidery, which originated in Ireland, became popular. This was known as Mountmellick work and was used on pillowcases and bedspreads.

The most popular type of embroidery during Queen Victoria's reign was canvaswork. It was known as Berlin woolwork because the printed patterns and the wools used to work them came originally from Germany. This form of

The Convalescent by Jules Emile Saintin. Victorian girls were expected to excel in refined accomplishments such as music and needlework, as part of their preparation for marriage.

embroidery was particularly suited to furnishings and it was produced in great abundance by enthusiastic Victorian needlewomen.

Although canvaswork designs were largely embroidered in wool, some areas might be worked in silk or in beads. From the mid-1850s onwards, it became common to work entire designs in beads, to the extent that beadwork on canvas developed into a form of embroidery in its own right. Because beadwork is so peculiar to this brief period it has a particular flavour of the age. The beads were generally made of glass and the colours have not faded over the years. We can, therefore, appreciate in their full glory any beadwork embroideries that survive, knowing that they look just as they did when first made.

In the last quarter of the nineteenth century Victorian taste began to change. By the mid-1870s the heavy, florid style of earlier times was giving way to a greater simplicity in architecture, furniture and decoration. The influence began to be felt both of the Japanese-inspired Aesthetic Movement and of the Arts and Crafts

Movement. The latter had its roots in William Morris's philosophy that honest design had to be true to its materials.

William Morris (1834–1896) was the most influential figure in the field of textiles in the second half of the nineteenth century and he had a significant effect on embroidery design. He felt that a piece of embroidery should look like a piece of embroidery, and should not attempt precise imitation of nature, masonry or lace. Most of Morris's designs were inspired by plant forms, but they were deliberately stylized and two-dimensional, rather than realistic. He insisted on using only natural fabrics and hated the artificial colours produced by analine dyes, preferring the softer, subtler tones of natural dyes. In 1861, Morris set up his own company Morris, Marshall, Faulkner and Co (later Morris and Co). All the embroideries produced by the firm were worked on linen with specially dyed silks and wools. By the 1890s home embroiderers could buy kits from the company complete with the appropriate yarns and with one corner worked as a guide.

Taste in needlework had certainly changed. Embroideries using fish scales and beetles' wings were no longer popular, and even Berlin woolwork was now rejected as tedious, giving no scope for the embroiderer's own artistic input.

In the late nineteenth century various groups and societies were set up which aimed to raise the standard of design and technique in embroidery. The most famous was the Royal School of Art Needlework, founded in London in 1872 and presided over by Queen Victoria's daughter, Princess Christian. (Art was dropped from the School's name in the 1920s.) The School's aim, as well as to raise standards, was to 'supply suitable employment for poor gentlefolk'. It became very prestigious and soon had a branch in Glasgow and agencies in other major cities in Britain as well as in Boston and Philadelphia in the United States. Leading artists, including Morris, Walter Crane and Edward Burne-Jones, designed embroideries especially for the Royal School.

Art needlework became as fashionable as Berlin woolwork had been in the past. Sun-

A panel depicting St Catherine (c. 1860), designed by William Morris in wool and silk embroidery.
Opposite: White silk embroidery (c. 1850) on satin.

flowers were a favourite emblem of the Aesthetic Movement and they, along with irises, lilies and daisies, bloomed abundantly in the new needlework designs. The flowers were worked in wool and silks in restrained colours on crash linen. Themes and techniques from the past were also used as sources for inspiration, including seventeenth-century crewelwork and peasant-style embroidery such as smocking. Smocked dresses were worn by both children and adults in artistic circles.

The concept of this book spans a period of 60 years and covers a wide variety of both needlework techniques and fashion in design. My aim has been to present a selection of projects that will give you just a taste of the most characteristic types of embroidery from this rich and fertile era.

Many of the threads and fabrics popular in Victorian times are no longer available, so I have suggested appropriate modern alternatives that will give an authentic look. I have also concentrated on designs suited to our modern lifestyle, which has meant avoiding pen-wipers, cigar cases and embroidered braces in favour of more useful items such as cushions, bedlinen, a table cloth, a footstool, pincushions and Christmas tree ornaments. I have also included samplers, pictures and boxes as well as clothing and accessories, such as some jet dress decoration, a lovely evening bag and suggestions for a pintucked baby robe. In a more frivolous vein, I could not resist adding a pattern for one of the most typical of all Victorian embroidery projects – a pair of Berlin woolwork slippers.

BEADWORK

The Englishwoman's Domestic Magazine provided its readers with a wide variety of patterns and designs, such as this design for a breakfast 'tray', to be worked in Berlin wool work. (From an issue in 1868.)

Opposite: Beadwork footstools sometimes took thousands of tiny beads to complete. Flowers were a favourite subjects of Victorian embroiderers, and used for every type of embroidery.

Beads featured widely in Victorian embroidery. Millions of them were sold and they were used to decorate garments, to trim braids or to decorate footstools, cushions and fire-screens. They were even used to cover piano stools, which must have been rather uncomfortable. Beads were incorporated into knitting and crochet and were made up into fringes for lampshades and bags. In short, they were used to decorate almost anything from watch pockets and braces to tea cosies and valances.

Beadwork requires an enormous number of beads. The tiny purse shown on page 19 took about 1,200, and the footstool (opposite) required 8,000 for the background alone.

For bead embroidery the beads were either sewn by hand or they were tamboured. Tambouring involves holding the fabric taut in a frame and using a fine hook, rather like a crochet hook, to work the stitches. For beadwork on canvas the beads were sewn on with either tent stitch or half cross stitch and designs were worked from charts similar to those used for Berlin woolwork. A piece might be worked entirely in beads, or wool was sometimes used for the background. Alternatively, the design might be mainly Berlin woolwork with beads used simply for highlights.

The beads required for beadwork are readily available today and are generally sold in boxes of approximately 600. Within each box there will be slight variations in the size of bead, but this will not affect the finished work. When working on canvas, make sure that the size of the bead matches the mesh of the canvas. If the beads are too large for the canvas holes they

will force the threads out of alignment and will not lie neatly.

Most types of beadwork require a beading needle. This is a particularly fine and flexible needle with a narrow eye, enabling it to pass easily through the hole in the bead. There are different thicknesses of needle to suit different sizes of bead but because of their narrow eyes, they are difficult to thread. It helps to wax the thread, by drawing it over a piece of candle or beeswax. It is a good idea not to cut off a length of cotton before attempting to thread the needle as the cotton may need to be trimmed several times before it is successfully threaded. Leave the yarn on the reel, thread the needle and then cut off the required length. You might even thread several needles on to the reel before beginning work, taking each off in turn with a suitable length of thread.

Use a strong, fine cotton or polyester thread in a colour that matches the beads, and use it double if possible. Always fasten thread ends securely. Start with a knot and, if working on canvas, take the yarn around a thread of the fabric and stitch into the knot. Finish off each length of thread firmly with back stitching and work a French knot into the stitches to give them extra strength.

F L O R A L   F O O T S T O O L

This is one of a pair of Victorian beadwork footstools. Floral designs such as this were a favourite subject of the era, for every type of embroidery. A border of tent stitch in black wool has been added to make the embroidery fit the footstool and to make it easier to mount.

Size
The finished beadwork is 10in (25cm) in diameter.

MATERIALS

(The footstool is worked with round beads of about $1/16$in (1.5mm) diameter.)

Beads in your choice of colours
Strong sewing thread in neutral or colours to match the beads
Beading needles
12-mesh double-thread canvas
Beeswax (to wax the thread). If beeswax is not easily available, an ordinary domestic wax candle can also be used.

ORDER OF STITCHING

Fold the canvas in half each way to find the centre. Baste along the fold lines using coloured thread. Work the design following the chart. The centre is indicated by arrows. Start in the centre. You can work the areas of the design in any order, but it is easier to work a patterned area first and then fill in the background around it. Use thread doubled if possible and work in either beaded half cross stitch or beaded tent stitch throughout. (Refer to page 120 for the techniques.) Do not mix the stitches as they will pull against each other.

If you prefer, the background can be worked in Berlin woolwork to make the beadwork stand out in relief. If the beadwork is in beaded half cross stitch, use half cross stitch for the background. If you are using beaded tent stitch then use tent stitch for the wool work.

Detail of Floral Footstool.

G O T H I C   C U S H I O N

The beadwork on this cushion probably began as part of a valance designed to fit along a mantelpiece or over a window. A later hand has stitched two pieces of border on to a velvet background. The centre line and the edges have been finished with a thick cord in toning colours. The advantage of using this type of design is that you can suit the number of repeats to the size of the cushion you want to make.

The medieval influence is found in much Victorian art, as seen here in the Gothic Cushion.

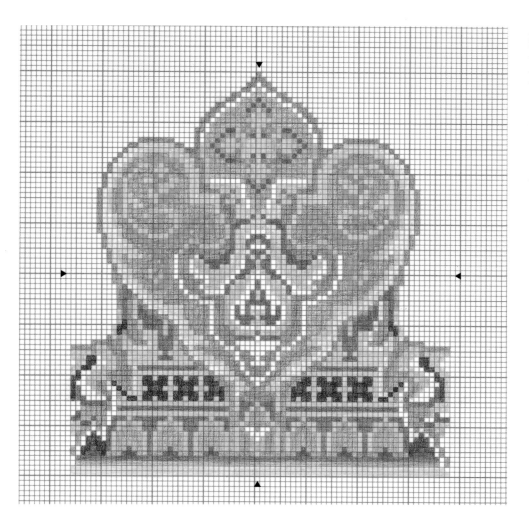

Left: Working chart for the beadwork motif. If you prefer, you can do the entire cushion front on canvas, working a background in woolwork first, then working the beadwork design afterwards. Use either half cross stitch or tent stitch for both embroidery and beadwork.

The design could also be used for a bag. Work two separate motifs, make them up into a bag, and finish with a cord stitched around the edges and along the top. For a special touch, you might attach a tassel to the bottom point.

Size

Approx 18 × 12 in (45 × 30cm)

MATERIALS

The cushion is worked in round beads of about $1/16$in (1.5mm) diameter.

Beads in your choice of colours

Strong sewing thread in neutral or colours to match the beads.
Beading needles
12-mesh double-thread canvas
Beeswax (to wax the thread)

ORDER OF STITCHING

Fold the canvas in half each way to find the centre. Baste along the fold lines using coloured thread. Work the design following the chart on this page. Use thread double if the hole in the bead is large enough. Use either beaded half cross stitch or beaded tent stitch throughout (refer to page 120). It is important that all stitches slant in the same direction.

JET-BEADED DRESS

Jet beads were fashionable in the second half of the nineteenth century both as jewellery and as decoration on clothing. Queen Victoria remained in mourning long after the death of the Prince Consort in 1861, and it was considered to be a compliment to her to wear these shiny black beads.

The jet industry received a further boost in the 1870s for a rather strange reason. Then, as now, fashion trends were led by Paris. After the crushing French defeat in the Franco-Prussian War in 1870–1871, Paris was left demoralized and close to starvation. Reflecting British interest in the situation, *The Englishwoman's Domestic Magazine* commented, in April 1871, on a side-effect that France's unhappy state had had on fashion:

'French ladies are better than they are generally believed to be and, during the time of distress and famine, fashion and frivolities were set aside. Those ladies whose duties kept them at home, and who did not wear the *ambulancière* costume, were never seen but in deepest mourning. Black cashmere or dull silk costumes, trimmed with crêpe and jet, are even now almost the only ones to be seen in Paris. Jet beads are fast coming into fashion again for trimmings. We have examined some new braids with very pretty patterns in small cut jet beads, and all the new passe-menterie trimmings for spring and summer mantles are beaded with jet. Even gloves have beaded ornaments on the back of the hand.'

Jet beads are not easily obtained today but faceted black beads are available and look as effective.

The dress pictured is in smooth panné velvet and is quite plain except for the neck front, which is embroidered in round-cut black glass beads. The design has been matched to the scooped neck of the garment, but it would work equally well on a high-necked dress.

Size
Approximate dimensions of the motif, 14 × 7in (35 × 18cm)

MATERIALS

Faceted black glass beads, 1/5in (5mm) diameter, approximately 450
Strong black thread
Crewel needle
Tissue paper, pencil
Embroidery frame (optional)

ORDER OF STITCHING

Trace the half design on folded tissue paper. Re-trace to obtain the complete design. Baste the tracing to the fabric.

Keep the thread fairly short, about 14in (35.5cm). Start with a knot, as this is safer than working a few back stitches. Stitch the beads along the drawn outlines using a double thread and either running stitch or back stitch. The stitches must be the same length as the diameter of the bead. If they are shorter, the beads will not lie in a straight line; if longer, the beads will slide about and wear the thread. If you use running stitch, the under stitches should be very tiny. Fasten off with two or three small back stitches, then work a French knot through the stitches.

Tear the tissue paper away carefully when all the bead embroidery has been completed.

Bead embroidery should be worked on garment pieces before they are made up for ease in working but it is also possible to bead a ready-made dress.

Opposite: Half of the floral motif is given here. Trace it on folded tracing paper, then re-trace to obtain the complete motif.

SILKEN BEADED PURSE

This small silk purse is worked with very small gold-coloured glass beads in a geometric repeat pattern. The back and front are the same, the design having been worked in one strip and then folded to make the bag. The embroiderer cleverly chose a fabric with a clear vertical line to guide the stitches. The design would look just as effective on a plain matt silk.

Size
4 × 3½in (10 × 9cm)

MATERIALS

Tiny round gold-coloured glass beads $\frac{1}{25}$in (1mm) diameter – approximately 1,200
Pale turquoise fabric 9 ×4½ in (23 × 12cm)
Strong fine thread in the background colour
Fine beading needles
Beeswax or candle (to wax thread)

ORDER OF STITCHING

Trace the design and transfer it to the fabric. Stitch the beads in place with back stitch, using a single thread in the needle.

Above: detail of the beaded purse.
Opposite: Small, beaded purses, shaped like Dorothy bags on a drawstring, were simple to make and usually matched the gown. Beads or gold-thread embroidery were used to embellish evening purses for a special effect.

SAMPLERS

Samplers date back at least to the seventeenth century, when professional embroiderers made them as a record of their stitches and designs and on these early samplers the stitching is often exceptionally fine. Later, as they learned to sew, children made samplers to practise their stitches. These examples usually feature pictures of birds, people, trees, flowers and buildings, but out of proportion to each other and often two-dimensional with no attempt at perspective.

By the nineteenth century samplers had become more simple, and often only cross stitch was used. Neatness of work was all important.

Samplers were also used as a means of teaching other lessons besides needlework and neatness. For example, they might take the form of multiplication tables or, of course, the alphabet. Many are designed around a biblical text or feature some moral lesson. The Victorians were obsessed with death and it was not unusual for a child of six or eight years old to make a sampler with words anticipating her own mortality, or commemorating a dead sibling.

In schools for the poor and in orphanages, girls destined for domestic service would learn to do all sorts of plain sewing and would sometimes work a sampler. This would usually be closely covered with alphabet letters of different sizes and types and often had a variety of borders. The alphabets were invaluable for marking household linen, as noted in a contemporary manual for the National Female Schools of Ireland: 'Marking in cross stitch, though very much superseded by the use of marking ink, is yet sufficiently useful, and is still so generally practised as to render a knowledge of the proper mode of doing so an indispensable part of the business of a National School for teaching plain-work.' Today, samplers are worked for pleasure or as a decorative way to mark an important family occasion.

FABRICS

Cross stitch samplers are always worked on evenweave fabric which dictates the rather formal and stylized patterns produced. The examples in this chapter, one recently made and two from the nineteenth century, are worked on fabrics of different thread count. The fabrics usually chosen for samplers today are Aida (11, 14 or 18 threads to 1in (2.5cm)); Hardanger fabric (22 threads to 1in (2.5cm)); and Linda (27 threads to 1in (2.5cm)). These are all cotton fabrics and are available in white or off-white. (The latter darkens quite quickly to a soft creamy beige.) Some are available in colours such as pink and blue, which might be used for birth samplers, or in holly green which is lovely for Christmas themes. Linen, which looks beautiful and is pleasant to work on, is also available in a variety of thread counts, but is comparatively expensive.

STITCHES AND PATTERNS

The samplers pictured in this chapter are all worked in simple cross stitch. When working, keep the stitches even and to ensure that the top threads of crosses lie in the same direction. The method for working cross stitch is on page 122.

'House and Garden' is a modern sampler designed on traditional Victorian themes and motifs. The working chart is on page 22.

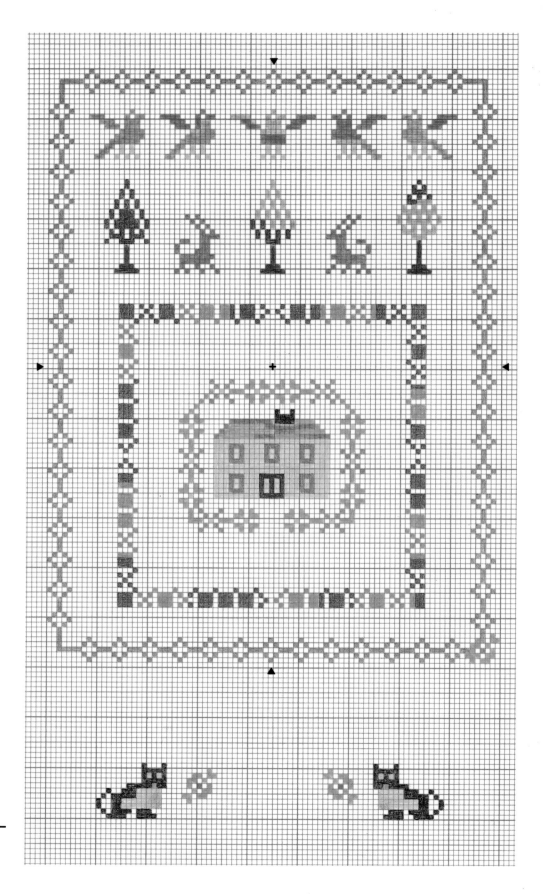

Today, samplers are worked for pleasure rather than as a task, as in the past. Traditional motifs, birds, deer, and the family cat are incorporated in this modern interpretation of a Victorian sampler.

HOUSE AND GARDEN SAMPLER

This is a modern sampler and represents a house surrounded by a flower garden, enclosed by a hedge. Outside is a forest, inhabited by deer and, above, a flock of birds fly in a blue sky. The deer and bird motifs are traditional and can sometimes be seen on old samplers.

Size

Sampler pictured measures 9 × 6¾in (23 × 17 cm).

MATERIALS

DMC stranded embroidery cotton, 1 skein each of the following colours:

- blue (809)
- shaded brown (105)
- yellow (743)
- shaded green (122)
- brown (801)
- light brown (841)
- shaded grey (53)
- shaded red (roof) (57)
- green (954)
- pink (963)
- lavender (210)
- blue (775)
- blue (792)

12 × 14in (30 × 35cm) of evenweave fabric, 27 threads to 1in (2.5cm)
Crewel embroidery needle
Embroidery frame

ORDER OF STITCHING

Following the chart and key, work the sampler in cross stitch. Use two strands of stranded cotton worked over two threads of the fabric for everything except the lettering, cats and tiny flowers. Work these in a single strand of cotton over one thread of fabric. A name can be worked centrally below the house, with the month and year above.

Detail from the House and Garden sampler.

23

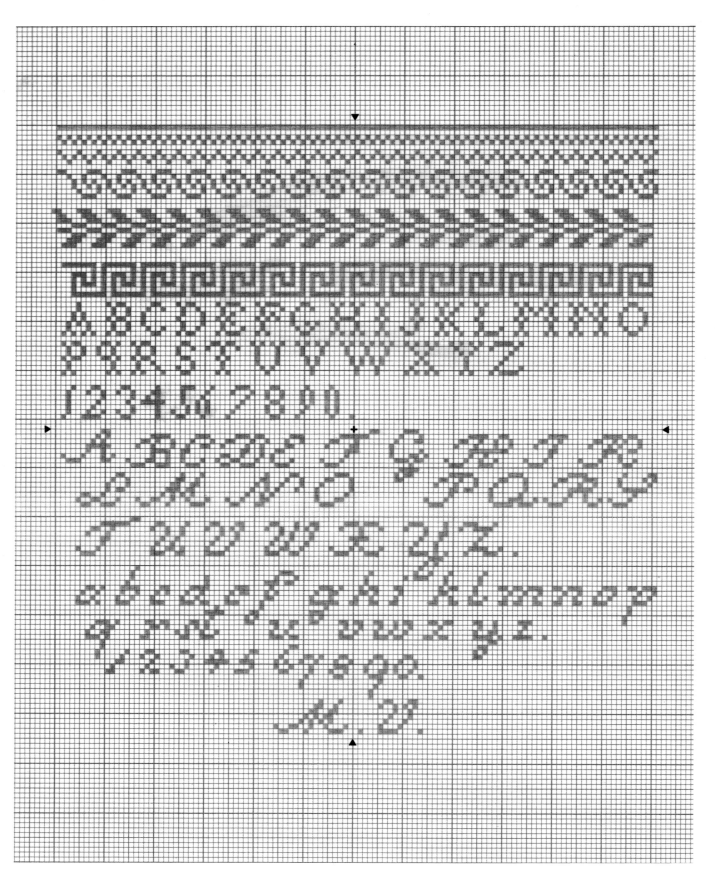

A L P H A B E T
S A M P L E R

This sampler has been worked on 13-mesh double-thread white canvas with an embroidery thread closely resembling Coton à Broder. Cross stitches are worked over one double thread of the canvas.

The canvas seems to have been specially made for samplers as it has a red and blue border. The design would work just as well on evenweave fabric with the woven border replaced with one of the patterns from the sampler. You can work the sampler following the original, or you may prefer to select different elements to create your own design. For example, a verse from one of your favourite poems could be combined with a double border of the wave pattern.

Like many 19th-century samplers, this one is made up of a variety of different border patterns and the alphabet is in several different styles. The working chart is on the opposite page.

F L O W E R   A N D   B I R D
M O T I F S

This delightful sampler was worked in 1865 by Eliza Manser who was a pupil at Dover Charity School. It is worked on a very closely-woven fabric (about 38 threads to the inch), and the stitches are made over two threads.

The sampler features alphabets on different scales, border patterns and various motifs — crowns, a gardener, a bird, stylized flowers in a pot, a castle and a church. At the bottom there are three larger motifs, two of flowers and one of a bird and flowers. These motifs have been abstracted for you to work. The whole design is surrounded by a border of stylized rosebuds. The sampler is mainly in cross stitch, but one lower case alphabet is in back stitch worked over two threads to form squares.

The details are taken from the Dover Charity School Sampler (opposite). Above, *Posy of Flowers*, top right, *Bird amid Flowers*, right, *Rose*.
Charts for these designs are overleaf.

Elizabeth Manser's sampler
was worked in 1865. As a
pupil at a charity school she
might well have been destined
for domestic service and would
have had to use her sewing
skills to mark household linens.

Detail from *Posy of Flowers* (see page 26). The chart (right) is indicated in colours that are keyed to the thread colours on the opposite page.

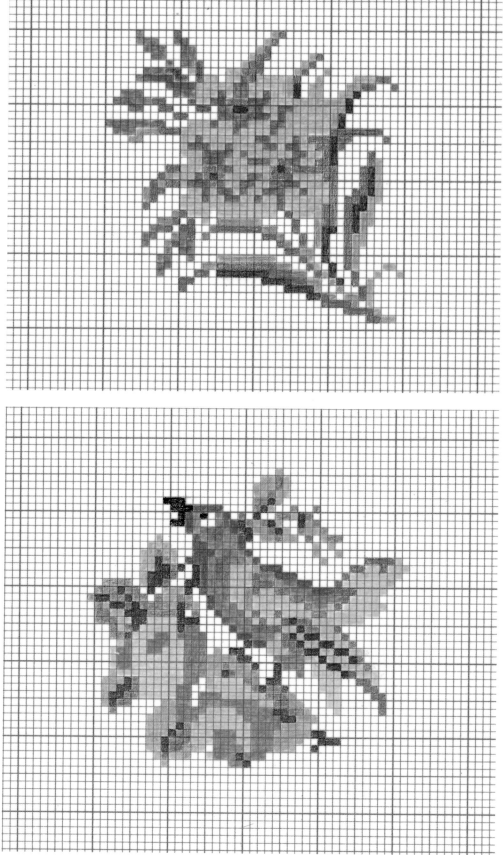

Detail from *Bird amid Flowers* (see page 26). The chart for working this design is on the right. Work the embroidery using the chart and the key to thread colours opposite. The chart for *Rose* is on the opposite page.

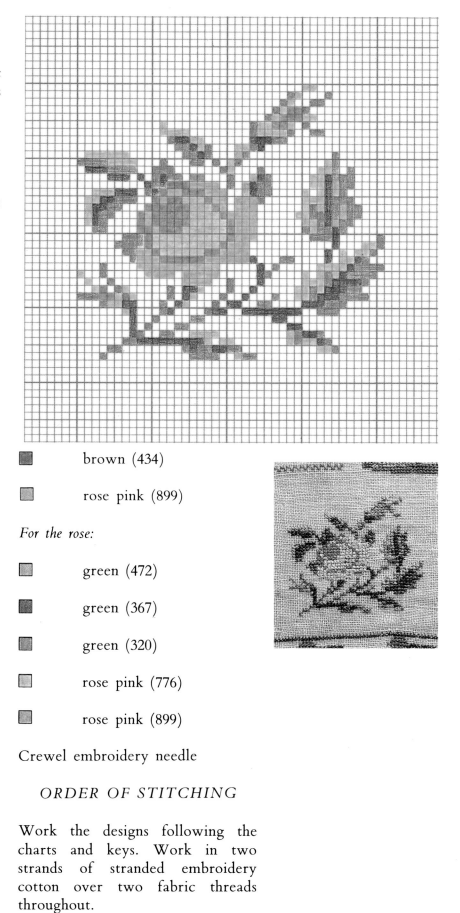

Size

This depends on the type of fabric chosen and the number of threads worked over.

MATERIALS

Evenweave fabric
DMC stranded embroidery cottons:

For the posy of flowers:

☐   green (472)

☐   green (3347)

☐   green (367)

☐   green (320)

☐   green (368)

☐   yellow (744)

☐   brown (921)

☐   rose pink (899)

For the bird amid flowers:

☐   green (472)

☐   green (3347)

☐   green (367)

☐   blue (813)

☐   blue (825)

☐   dark grey (413)

☐   light grey (762)

☐   beige (738)

☐   light brown (436)

☐   brown (434)

☐   rose pink (899)

For the rose:

☐   green (472)

☐   green (367)

☐   green (320)

☐   rose pink (776)

☐   rose pink (899)

Crewel embroidery needle

ORDER OF STITCHING

Work the designs following the charts and keys. Work in two strands of stranded embroidery cotton over two fabric threads throughout.

BERLIN WOOLWORK

Berlin woolwork was the most popular kind of needlework in the second half of the nineteenth century. For centuries canvaswork had been practised with the patterns drawn out onto the canvas but in the early 1800s a German printer developed the idea of printing designs on to squared paper, which the embroiderer could copy. Each coloured square represented one stitch on the canvas. By the 1830s vast quantities of these patterns were being imported into England from Germany, together with the wools for working them, hence the name Berlin woolwork. Soon patterns were being designed and produced in both England and America, and were frequently given away with magazines.

So popular was Berlin woolwork that examples of it were to be found everywhere in the Victorian home. It was used for covering stools and chairs and as pictures, for bell pulls, tiebacks, valances, tablecloths and carpets.

Although samplers exist showing a wide variety of stitches for Berlin woolwork, most of the embroidery was carried out in tent stitch, cross stitch or half cross stitch.

Double and single thread canvases of different weights were used, including a very fine silk canvas which was attractive enough for the background to be left unworked.

All three designs given in this chapter are worked in either half cross stitch or tent stitch. Canvas is available in white, which is best for pale colours, or antique, which is best for mid or dark colours. The mesh of the canvas refers to the number of threads to 1in (2.5cm). For example, 12-mesh canvas has 12 threads and 11 holes to 1in (2.5cm). It is always best to work in a frame.

Hundreds of pairs of slippers must have been embroidered for husbands, fathers and uncles during Queen Victoria's reign and Berlin woolwork was the favourite medium.

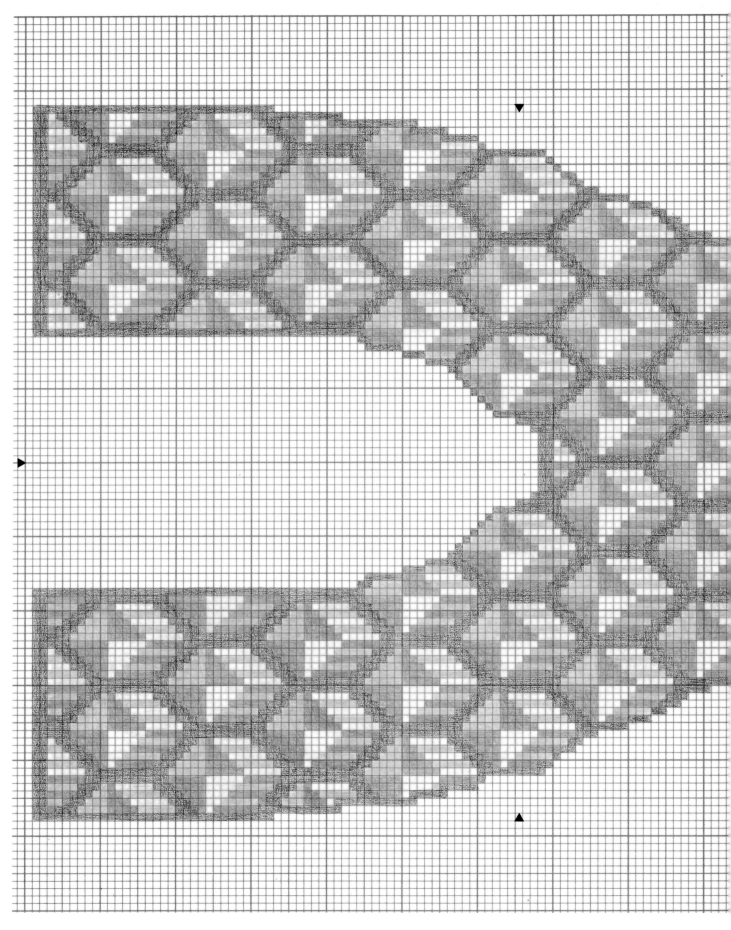

S L I P P E R S

Geometric repeat patterns like this one are particularly suitable for slippers as you simply draw out the slipper to size on the canvas. Then, starting at the centre front, repeat the pattern until you have covered the shape. The slippers have been lined with a thin felt and the edges finished with a cord. The soles are felt, but could equally well be of chamois leather.

Size
The pattern is for an English man's size 8 (US size 42).

MATERIALS

DMC tapestry wools:

◼   black – 7 skeins

◻   light grey (7282) – 2 skeins

◻   pink (7759) – 2 skeins

◻   burgundy (7139) – 2 skeins

11-mesh double thread canvas
Tapestry needle
Tapestry frame

ORDER OF STITCHING

Draw out the slipper shape to the correct size on the canvas. Following the chart and key, work the pattern all over the drawn shape. Start working at the centre front. Half cross stitch is probably better than tent stitch for this design as it produces a thinner and more pliable fabric for making up into slippers. Work a second slipper; finish the edges with a decorative cord.

The chart for the slippers is on the opposite page. A detail of the pattern is above.

C H R Y S A N T H E M U M
C U S H I O N

This design was based on a pretty motif of oriental-style chrysanthemums found on some Victorian china. Following the chart and key, work the design in half cross stitch.

Size
13 × 13in (33 × 33cm)

MATERIALS

DMC tapestry wools:

☐ white – 7 skeins

▨ blue (7797) – 2 skeins

▨ dark blue (7796) – 2 skeins

☐ gold (7782) – 1 skein

▨ green (7382) – 1 skein

▨ light brown (7463) – 1 skein

▨ brown (7801) – 1 skein

☐ light peach/brown (7176) – 1 skein

▨ rust (7360) – 1 skein

▨ dark rust (7303) – 1 skein

☐ peach (7175) – 1 skein

11-mesh canvas in antique colour
Tapestry needle
Tapestry frame

The design and colouring of this cushion was taken from the pattern on a set of Victorian china by Ridgeways called *Fantasia*.

T U R K I S H - S T Y L E
C A S E

This case is worked in two shades of a very fine wool and two shades of twisted embroidery cotton. The contrast between the soft matt wool and the shiny twisted cotton gives textural interest. The pattern, reminiscent of Turkish carpets, which were a very popular Victorian theme, was adapted from a border design for a table cover, published in a magazine of the 1870s. The case is backed and the top edge is bound with red felt, but you may prefer to work both sides of the case to match.

The Turkish influence can be seen reflected in Victorian paintings, ceramics, carpets, furnishings and in embroidery. Stylized minarets form the design here.

Size
6½ × 3in (16.5 × 7.5cm)

MATERIALS

The following quantities are sufficient to work both sides of the spectacles case.

DMC Broder Médicis wool: ·

■ red (8127) – 4 skeins

■ pale tangerine (8129) – 2 skeins

DMC Coton Perlé:

■ turquoise (991) 1 skein

■ turquoise (993) – 1 skein

15-mesh single thread canvas
Tapestry needle
Tapestry frame

ORDER OF STITCHING

Following the chart and key, work the case front in tent stitch. (Tent stitch is better than half cross stitch as it fills in the canvas more successfully and gives the work more body.) Use three strands of the wool together. Use a single strand of the Coton Perlé. Work a second side in the same way.

G O L D E N   B E E   B O X

Canvas lace was a fashionable technique for bordering pieces of Berlin woolwork, and numerous repeat patterns for it can be found on some Victorian samplers. *The Englishwoman's Domestic Magazine* offered a diagram sheet for 'The Chantilly Lambrequin for mantelpiece, what-not and bracket borders'.

The open lacy effect of the box is created by using cross stitch in a fine black thread on a white canvas. The lid of the box is worked in two different thicknesses of black thread and a fine gold machine embroidery thread. The bee in the centre is embroidered in gold and bronze beads. The design would work equally well as a picture. Alternatively, it could be enlarged to make a table centre,

make it into a clutch bag by extending the border to surround a row of bees.

Size
4¼ × 4¼in (10.06 × 10.06cm)

MATERIALS

Stranded embroidery cotton, black – 1 skein (shown grey)
Appleton's crewel wool, black – 1 skein (shown black)
Madeira machine embroidery thread no.40, gold (8) – 1 spool
18-mesh single thread white canvas
Round bronze and gold beads
Tapestry needle
Beading needle

ORDER OF STITCHING

Following the chart and key and using a single thread of black or gold yarn as appropriate, work the border design, centre panel and bee's wings in cross stitch over two threads of canvas. Fill in the scallops around the outer edge of the border with upright cross stitch worked with three strands of the gold yarn over two threads of canvas. Sew on the beads for the insect's body with one or two strands of black stranded cotton, using back stitch. For this you should ignore the threads of the canvas and stitch the beads where necessary to make a pleasing shape. (It is best to use back stitch to sew on these beads rather than beaded tent or half cross stitch, either of which would give too rigid and open an effect.) Finally, add the feelers in back stitch with a single strand of cotton.

Below and opposite:
In contrast to the strict geometry of the rest of the design, the bee's body is worked freehand, without regard for the threads of the canvas.

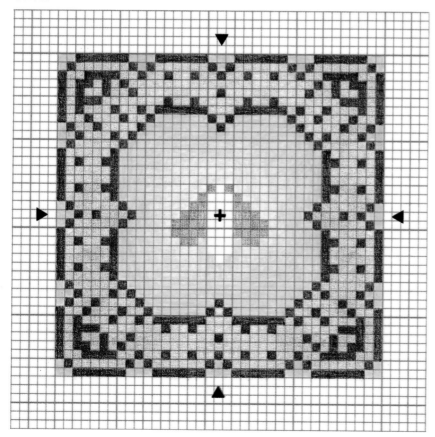

SURFACE EMBROIDERY

Although Berlin woolwork was the most popular form of needlecraft from the 1860s onwards, ordinary surface embroidery did not lose its appeal. Many of the items that were decorated with Berlin woolwork were considered equally suitable for other forms of embroidery.

Flowers, both stylized and naturalistic, were the most frequently used motifs. Embroiderers could either draw up their own designs or they could use one of the numerous patterns offered by magazines. Even the latter gave scope for personal interpretation in the choice of threads, fabrics and colours. Fabrics used included silk, satin, velvet, sateen, cotton, felt and leather. Yarns ranged from stranded silk or cotton, twisted silk and wool to metal threads.

Opposite: Many Victorian women owned a soft, lightweight stole like this. It would have been worn for a little warmth with low-necked dresses.

Pretty designs of flowers, leaves and ribbons were popular throughout Europe during the 19th century and were often used for special, embroidered greetings cards.

G E O R G E T T E   S T O L E

The embroidery on this original Victorian stole consists of a simple repeated border design with two lines of equally simple flowers above. Only three colours are used – yellow, green and lilac – and just two stitches, satin and stem stitch. The secret of the success of this piece of embroidery lies in the perfect neatness and accurate placing of the stitches and the strict uniformity of the design.

The stole has hemstitching along the ends and down the sides. Lace has then been applied to the side edges right up to the hemstitching, and the surplus fabric has been cut away very close to the stitching. The ends of the stole have been decorated with a long, silky, knotted fringe.

The design can be adapted to fit any bought chiffon scarf by adjusting the number of repeats to fit the width. Alternatively, you might prefer to make your own scarf, using a soft, fine fabric. It is advisable to finish the edges with a hemstitched border or a rolled edge before working the embroidery to prevent the fabric from fraying.

MATERIALS

Long scarf in georgette or chiffon
Madeira stranded pure silk thread, 1 packet each of the following colours:

yellow (0113)
green (1408)
lilac (0801)

Fine embroidery crewel needle
Embroidery frame

ORDER OF STITCHING

It is easier to work an unstable fabric such as georgette in a frame, especially when accuracy in positioning the motifs is as important as it is here.

Work both ends of the scarf in the same way. Trace the design and transfer it to the fabric, starting with the border. The border motifs should be touching at the bottom of the stems. Then position the motifs for the row of larger flowers, spacing the flowers above and in between the top of each 'point' of the border. Place the final row of small flowers above and in between the previous row.

Use two strands of stranded silk throughout for the embroidery. Following the colours of the trace-off patterns, work the leaves and flowers in satin stitch, working the stitches across each petal and diagonally towards the centre of each leaf. Changing the direction of the stitches in this way helps to give light and shade to the embroidery. Work the stems and central vein of each leaf in stem stitch. Stitches should be kept even and fairly small.

Detail of the georgette stole on page 41. The trace-off pattern is on the opposite page.

Trace these full-sized motifs and transfer them to the fabric. The larger motif goes along the border while the single flowers are arranged as shown on page 41.

43

ROSES AND FORGET-ME-NOTS

In Victorian homes it was not only windows that were heavily draped with fabric. Mantelpieces and shelves would also frequently be decorated with a valance. This delightful example is in black sateen, beautifully worked in a design of naturalistic flowers. It features three sprays of roses and forget-me-nots, the two side panels being identical except for a change in colouring, and the central section showing a different arrangement of the same flowers. The finishing touches are the cord and tassels which pick up the colours of the embroidery.

The bag has been worked on black satin and the design is a copy of the left hand panel of the valance. The same stitches are used as in the original and the colours have also been matched as closely as possible. If you wish to work the whole valance, use the bag pattern for the side panels and add extra flowers to make a slightly larger centre panel. You can vary the colours slightly from panel to panel if desired.

Size

8 × 8½in (20 × 22cm)

MATERIALS

Madeira stranded silk, 1 packet each of the following colours:

pink (0306)
maroon (0811)
light blue (1710)
slate blue (1706)
blue-green (1704)
cream (2014)
green (1407, 1409, 1508 and 1510)
brown (2008)
gold (2213)

9 × 20in (23 × 60cm) firmly-woven black satin fabric
Fine embroidery crewel needles

This valance, used here over a mirror, would have been intended originally to edge a shelf or fit over a small window.

The design of naturalistic flowers on this evening bag was taken directly from the left-hand panel of the valance (see picture left, page 44). The trace-off pattern is above, left. Follow the colours indicated on the pattern for threads.

ORDER OF STITCHING

Trace the design and transfer it to the fabric. Work the embroidery following the colours of the trace-off pattern. Use a single strand of thread unless otherwise stated. The leaves and forget-me-nots are worked in satin stitch. The buds are worked in long chain stitches. The red stems are in stem stitch as are the stems of the forget-me-nots to the left of the centre. All other stems are worked in split stitch using two strands of thread.

V E L V E T C A P

This smoking cap which would probably have been made as a present for a husband, father or favourite uncle. There might also have been a jacket with matching embroidery. There is no call for special outfits for smoking these days, but this soft pillbox shape with its floral embroidery and long matching tassel would delight a young girl.

The embroiderer of the original Victorian piece worked quickly to create an effect, and the stitching is not particularly good. However, the overall impression is very attractive. The cap is lined with quilted blue silk. The embroidery is two simple garlands of flowers and leaves, one surrounding the top of the cap, the other a repeat pattern for the band (see trace-off patterns on pages 48–49). This repeat pattern could be used around the bottom of a drawstring bag or on the flap of a clutch purse. Either pattern could be adapted to edge a bolero jacket.

The fabric for the cap in the picture is wine-red velvet and the yarn used for embroidery is a twisted silk thread which shows up well on the pile fabric. Only three yarn colours were used, a space-dyed green mix, pale blue and yellow. Coton Perlé no.8 is a good substitute for silk and is available in space-dyed and plain colours.

This pincushion is made on a box with a padded, satin fabric lid, edged with cord. The pinked valance is made of embroidered, white cricketing flannel. Ribbon ruchings cover the box and tassels add decoration.

Opposite: Make a pattern for a pillbox hat by cutting sides in paper, overlap ends, pin to fit. Use pinned circle to cut hat top adding ½in (12mm).

46

Size
The crown of the cap is 7in (17.5cm) in diameter and the sides are 3½in (9cm) deep. The cap circumference of 24in (60cm).

MATERIALS

13 × 25in (32.5 × 78cm) of richly-coloured dress-weight velvet fabric DMC Coton Perlé no.8, 1 skein each of the following colours:

space-dyed green (92)
sky blue (809)
yellow (727)
Medium-sized crewel needle

As well as being adept in decorative needlework, Victorian girls and their mothers were also skilled at dressmaking and made some of their own clothes as well as shirts, waistcoats, etc., for fathers and husbands. *The Song of the Shirt* is a detail from a painting by Frank Holl (1845–1888).

ORDER OF STITCHING

Trace the design and transfer the garland for the crown of the cap and the repeat band for the sides to the fabric. Work the embroidery, following the colours shown on the trace-off patterns. Work the flowers in satin stitch with the stitches lying along the length of the petal. Work French knots for the centres. Work the leaves in long-and-short stitch, taking the stitches along the length of the leaf and slightly outwards from the central vein. Work the stems last, using a single row of stem stitch and taking the line part of the way along the centre of the larger leaves to create the central vein. When you have made up the cap, it can be decorated with a covered button or a tassel on the crown, made from the same threads as the embroidery.

Trace the circular garland above for the crown of the smoking cap. Trace the band motif on the opposite page and trace on to the fabric twice so that the ends meet.

FLORAL GREETINGS

The giving of greeting cards was almost as popular a pastime in the nineteenth century as it is today. Hand-embroidered cards make delightful keepsakes, giving a flavour of times past, and flowers are a particularly appropriate choice of motif. The Victorians were very interested in the language of flowers, so the choice of flowers for a card usually had an added significance. Pansies, for example, were for thoughts, and roses had a variety of meanings according to their

This St Valentine's Day card would probably have been worked for a fiancé as Victorian girls would be unlikely to send messages of love to a man who had not indicated his marital intentions. Greeting cards of all kinds were ornate with lace paper, silver lace and ribbons.

colour. Red roses were for love, while yellow ones signified infidelity or fading love. A single rose stood for simplicity.

Both the designs shown here are worked with two strands of pure silk thread on silk fabric, but stranded cotton threads on a cotton or linen fabric could also be used. When the embroideries have been completed, mount them in cream or parchment-coloured cards made specially for the purpose, to give an antique look. If a piece of soft fabric or thin wadding is placed behind the work this will give it a softer, padded look. Cut the wadding to the size and shape of the opening in the mount (in this case, an oval).

In the language of flowers, red roses symbolized love; yellow represented infidelity.

PANSY

Size

Design fits an oval 4 × 3⅛in (10 × 8cm)

MATERIALS

Madeira stranded silk thread, 1 packet each of the following colours:

lavender (0901, 0902 and 0903)
yellow (0114)
green (1311 and 1704)
black

Piece of white or cream silk fabric

ORDER OF STITCHING

Trace the design and transfer it to the fabric. The embroidery can be worked in a frame or in the hand, as you prefer. Using two strands of thread throughout, work the design following the colours of the trace-off pattern. The flower and bud are worked in long-and-short stitch. The leaves are in satin stitch, worked diagonally towards the central vein in each case. The stems are in stem stitch, two lines for the main stem and a single line for the secondary one.

BRIAR ROSE
Size
Design for an oval 4 × 3⅛in (10 × 8cm)

MATERIALS

Madeira stranded silk thread, 1 packet each of the following colours:

rose pink (0503, 0504 and 0506)
yellow (0114)
green (1311 and 1704)
Piece of white or cream silk fabric (large enough to be held in an embroidery frame, if used)
Fine embroidery crewel needle
Embroidery frame (optional)

ORDER OF STITCHING

Trace the design and transfer it to the fabric. Work the embroidery in a frame or in the hand, as you prefer. Using two strands of thread throughout, work the design following the colours of the trace-off patterns.

The petals of the flower are in long-and-short stitch, with the centre worked in French knots.

The rosebud is worked in satin stitch. The leaves are in satin stitch, worked diagonally towards the centre, as for the pansy. The whole of each leaf is worked with one strand of each of the greens to give a subtle blend of colour. The stems are in stem stitch; the main one has two rows and the subsidiary one is a single line.

If you are working in a frame, you will need to slacken off the fabric when making the French knots in the flower centre.

This intricate St Valentine's Day card might have been sent by a man to a girl he admired as an indication of his concern that she was oblivious to his affections.

HANDKERCHIEF FOR A LADY

Flowers are again the theme for this delicate handkerchief with its limited palette of pale colours. The bold, simple design is enhanced by the contrast between the heavy twisted yarn and the fine silk on which it is worked. The design is composed of a central garland made up of four repeats of two flowers and two sprays of leaves with a repeated corner motif. The colours have been varied for different flowers so that, for example, two of the large corner roses are pink while the other two are cream. The edge is scalloped and finished with buttonhole stitch.

This is a very adaptable design. It could be repeated to make a dressing table mat or it could be used for a tea tablecloth. For this, you could create a large central garland by increasing the number of repeats and using the corner motifs just as they are. Change the fabric and yarn to suit the purpose of the embroidery.

Size
13 × 13in (32.5 × 32.5cm)

MATERIALS

16in (40cm) – square of off-white fine silk fabric
DMC Coton Perlé no.8 thread, 1 skein each of the following colours:
shaded green (94)
cream (712)
pink (818)
Fine embroidery crewel needle

ORDER OF STITCHING

Buttonhole-stitch the edges of the fabric. Trace the design and transfer it to the fabric. Following the colours of the trace-off pattern, work the embroidery. The large roses are in satin stitch. Work each petal separately and change the direction of the stitches in each case to give an effect of light and shade. The other solid flowers, buds and leaves are also in satin stitch. Take the stitches across each petal or leaf, working along the length from end to end. The star-shaped flowers are worked in single straight stitches and all the stems are worked in long back stitches.

Time has faded the bright colours of the original embroidery on this handkerchief, but the design is still well-defined because of the contrast between the filmy fabric and the texture of the thread.

F L O W E R F R A M E

Embroidery patterns in Victorian magazines sometimes suggested incorporating gold and silver threads in the design. Young ladies would make Bible covers in black velvet embroidered with gold braid, gold thread and black silk, or prayer book covers in violet silk worked in silver thread and cord.

The picture mount here uses metallic thread but is much more restrained, reflecting the influence of Art Needlework at the end of the century. The design is a repeat pattern of stylized flowers and twining leaves.

The photograph itself has interesting connections with embroidery history. It shows Elizabeth Wardle who was famous for her embroidery. She was married to a silk dyer and lived in Leek in Staffordshire, where she founded a group of lady embroiderers who carried out a great deal of ecclesiastical work. Their work often showed the influence of William Morris, who was a friend of Elizabeth's husband, William Wardle. There was an additional connection, in that Elizabeth's brother was employed by Morris. In the photograph, she appears to be embroidering a piece of Morris fabric. On the back of the frame is a hand-written label which reads 'Grandmother in Embroidered Frame', and another hand has added 'For Bridget'.

The picture mount is worked on a fairly thick beige silk, with flowers in shades of cream, peach and coral, and leaves and stems in shades of golden brown. Metallic gold thread outlines the petals.

This picture of Elizabeth Wardle, a well-known Victorian embroiderer, is set within a padded mount worked in an all-over design of flowers in silk, outlined in metallic thread.

Size

10 × 12in (25 × 30cm)

MATERIALS

Beige, matt silky fabric (such as taffeta)
Madeira stranded silks, 1 packet each of the following colours:

peach (0403)
coral (0402)
cream (0214)
brown/gold (2209, 2210 and 2114)
Madeira Metallic Embroidery Thread no.5 (5012)

Fine embroidery crewel needle
Embroidery frame (optional)

ORDER OF STITCHING

Trace the design (see note), and transfer it to the fabric. Work the embroidery following the colours of the trace-off pattern. Use two strands of stranded silk throughout. The stems are worked in either stem or outline stitch. The leaves and larger petals are in long-and-short stitch and the smaller petals are in satin stitch. Work the stems, leaves and flowers (except for the centres) in stranded silk. Next, work around the petals, using a single strand of the lightest leaf shade to couch down the gold thread. Finally, work the flower centres in stranded silk.

The Victorians were great inventors and loved gadgets as this elaborate embroidery frame shows.

The top, left-hand quarter of the mount pattern is given here. Trace this on folded tissue paper and then re-trace until you have the entire design.

FRUIT AND FLOWERS

This table runner reflects the more restrained taste of the latter part of the nineteenth century. The design of intertwining stylized fruit, flowers and leaves is worked in crewel wool on calico. The colouring, in brown and dull gold, is typical of this time when more brightly coloured embroidery was going out of fashion. The stitches include satin stitch, French knots, square filling stitch and stem stitch. Stem stitch was very popular for this type of work and is sometimes called South Kensington stitch, in a reference to the birthplace of the new 'artistic' taste.

This piece of embroidery might also have been a trial design for bordering a curtain or bedcover. You could make it up in either of these ways, choosing colours to match your room scheme, or you could use part of it to make a cushion cover. The pattern has been adapted to make a repeat design.

'Look at my antimacassar!' exclaims the dismayed Victorian lady. Antimacassars were embroidered cloths, used on chair and sofa backs to protect the fabric from macassar oil, which men used on their hair. Imported from an island off Indonesia, the oil was said to promote hair growth.

Size
As required, using repeats

Embroidery crewel needle
Embroidery frame

MATERIALS

Sufficient calico to make up the article of your choice
Appleton's crewel wool, 1 skein each of the following colours:
brown (955)
old gold (475)

ORDER OF STITCHING

Trace the pattern and transfer it to the fabric. Work the embroidery following the colours of the trace-off pattern using two strands of wool throughout, except for the small French knots in the square

Scale up the pattern half again for working in crewel wool. Use the pattern as it is for working in stranded, embroidery cotton.

trellis for which a single thread should be used. The stems are in padded satin stitch with the leaves in stem stitch. The petals of all the flowers are also stem stitch. The centres of the smaller open flowers are French knots with leafy sprays in either satin stitch or outlined in stem stitch with a filling of individual cross stitches. The leaves at the base of the closed flowers are in the same stitches as before. The central, folded petals of the large flower are emphasized with a double row of stem stitch, and at its heart there is an area of squared filling stitch. The fruit is outlined in stem stitch, and the filling is of lines of dull gold wool closely couched in the same colour with alternating lines of individual cross stitches.

P A I S L E Y
T A B L E
C L O T H

In the last quarter of the nineteenth century there was a fashion for Anglo-Indian work. Cotton fabrics were specially printed with designs based on Indian shawls, ready for embroidery. Although there was no scope for the embroiderer to adapt the pattern herself, some creative skill was involved in choosing which colours to use. This unfinished paisley cloth shows the wonderfully rich effect that could be created. The colours have obviously been chosen with great care and the subtle shading of the paisley motifs gives vitality to the work. The background and some areas of the pattern have been left unworked, so that the dense stitching of the design stands out in interesting relief against the smooth cloth. As the fabric is rather thin, and because the embroiderer only intended to work a border on it, she has basted the fabric on to a fine wool in the same red as the background.

The unfinished areas of the pattern show the extent to which personal interpretation could influence such a work. The garish two-dimensional original has been turned, by a clever choice of colours, into a work of art. You could create the same sort of effect in your embroidery by using a cheap Indian bedspread or cushion square as the basis for your stitchery.

Detail of the paisley cloth (shown opposite). A rich variety of stitches has been used to decorate the fabric and this is a technique that adapts well to modern printed fabrics.

ORDER OF STITCHING

The stitches used are long-and-short stitch, stem stitch, French knots, lazy daisy stitch, satin stitch, fly stitch, braid stitch, basket stitch and herringbone stitch. The last three are border stitches and together, make up the thick scrolling stems which weave in and out of the paisley motifs. The outer edges are herringbone stitch, inside them are bands of closely-worked basket stitch and in the centre is a line of braid stitch. The flowers are in satin stitch with French knot cen-

tres. The centre section of each paisley design is long-and-short stitch, surrounded by braid stitch, stem stitch or fly stitch. Some motifs are additionally ornamented with French knots. The leaves and the outer edges of the paisley patterns are lazy daisy stitch.

Most of the embroidery on the table cloth is worked with two strands of stranded silk, with one or two exceptions. The lines of stem stitch defining the shape of the paisley motifs, and the satin stitch on the flowers, are worked with four strands of silk.

Right: Cheap, printed fabric served as a basis for some beautiful, creative embroidery. *Opposite*: Entitled *Going to the Party*, this book illustration shows the girl on the left proudly wearing a shawl which might have been imported from India. These shawls were costly and much in demand. Cheaper, printed versions were produced in Scotland, bringing them within the reach of less wealthy women.

WHITEWORK

The type of embroidery at which the Victorians most excelled was whitework, which included various types of white embroidery on white linen, cotton or muslin. It was carried out by both professional and amateur needlewomen, and numerous examples of their work can still be found in antique shops and markets. Whitework was used mainly for bed and table linen and for clothes.

The most delicate work was the beautiful Ayrshire embroidery worked on muslin and used for baby clothes, fine shirts and underwear. This very high quality work combined areas of drawn thread fillings with needle-made lace and crisp surface embroidery in intricate floral patterns. It originated in Scotland where it was produced on a cottage industry basis. The pay was appalling and the work ruinous to the eyes.

As the century progressed, machine-made broderie anglaise, embroidery and lace became available and the Ayrshire industry declined. However, beautiful baby clothes, tucked and embroidered, continued to be made largely by hand, with the addition of bought trimmings. The bodice and sleeves were embroidered and often there would be an elaborate panel down the front of the skirt as well. Pintucks were a favourite additional decoration.

Today there is increasing interest in making similar heirloom garments for a son or daughter, grandchild or godchild. The work is very rewarding and not at all arduous. The highly decorated area can be confined to the bodice front and sleeves, and the skirt can be simply ornamented with rows of pintucks and feather stitching. You can use a commercial paper pattern of your own choice for a christening robe or a baby's dress, allowing extra fabric for working pintucks.

Above and opposite: Although Ayrshire was the finest type of whitework, the later Mountmellick embroidery was just as pleasing. It was used mainly for bedroom furnishings.

RIBBON-TIED CHRISTENING ROBE

This pretty design is open across the top of the neck and sleeves and is fastened with ribbons, which makes it easy to put on and take off.

MATERIALS

Fine cotton lawn
2⅛yds (2m) of ½in (1cm)-wide lace insertion, with two decorated edges
2¼yds (2m) of ⅛in (3mm)-wide white doublefaced ribbon
White stranded embroidery cotton
Fine needles

ORDER OF WORKING
Bodice:

Trace the pattern for the bodice (see page 75) and mark the position of the pintucks and cutting lines for the lace insertion on the fabric. Cut out the bodice. Cut along the lines for the insertion and make a ¹/₁₆in (4mm) hem on the raw edges, on the wrong side of the work. On the right side of the work, sew the lace

in place with small running stitches, so that there is a ¹/₆in (4mm) space between the two hemmed edges.

Make the pintucks and press them flat towards the sides of the garment.

Work the embroidery with two strands of stranded embroidery cotton, starting from the centre. Work four equally-spaced lazy daisy flowers in a vertical line and a line of feather stitching along the inner edge of each of the first pair of tucks. Work chain stitch along the inner edges of each of the new pair of tucks, followed by French knots, then feather stitch.

Sleeves:

Trace the pattern (see page 74) and mark the position of the pintucks and cutting lines. Cut out the sleeves. Cut along the cutting lines, hem and sew on lace. Make pintucks where indicated. Make a ¹/₅in (5mm) hem along the top edge of each sleeve and trim with lace to match. Work a line of feather stitching just outside each edge of the lace and then work lazy daisy flowers between each pair of lace lines.

When the garment is finished, sew a length of lace along the top of the front and back and add ribbons to tie over the shoulders and down the sleeves.

Opposite: Two bodice and sleeve designs inspired by nineteenth-century christening robes.

Below: Early Ayrshire work, like this muslin bonnet, shows the high standard of intricate stitchery and design that was achieved.

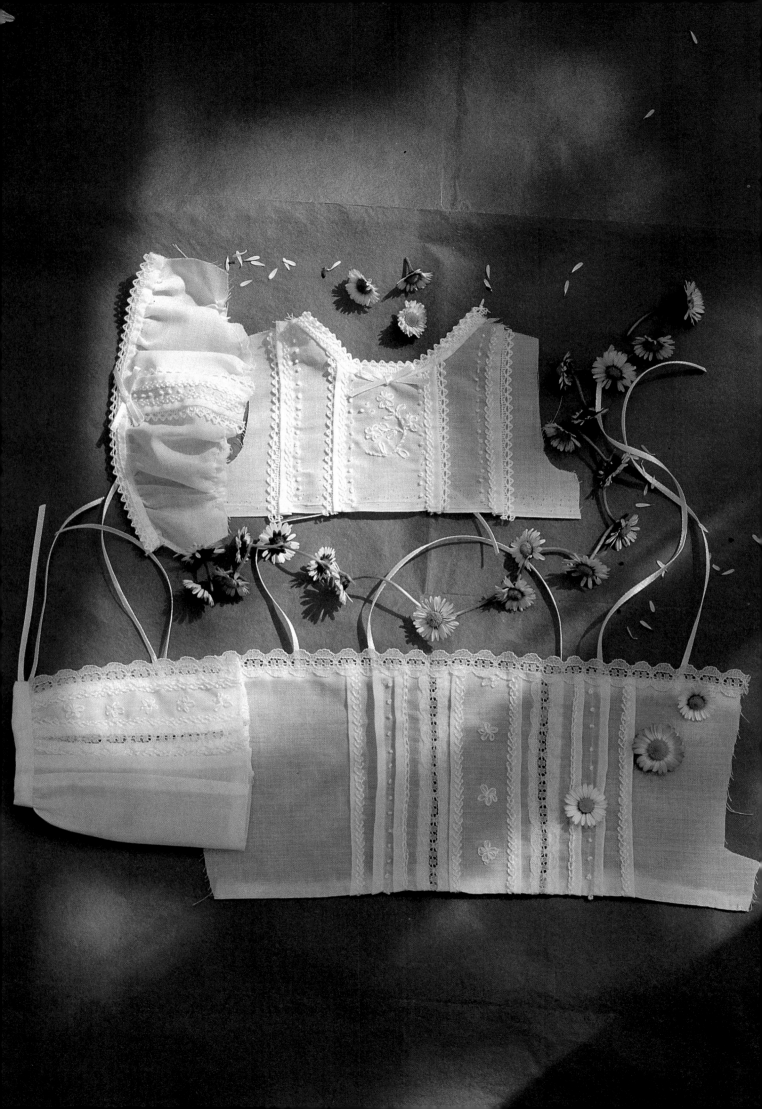

R O U N D - N E C K E D C H R I S T E N I N G   R O B E

The instructions given here are for pintucking and embroidering the bodice and sleeves of a round-necked robe.

MATERIALS

Paper pattern of christening robe
Fine cotton lawn
1⅛yd (1m) of ¼in (6mm)-wide lace edging
¾yd (70cm) of ⅛in (3mm)-wide white doublefaced satin ribbon
White stranded embroidery cotton
Fine needles

The Return from the Christening, a painting by Hubert Salenti. The baby is resplendent in a beautiful embroidered robe (similar to the one shown opposite), bonnet and veil, all richly trimmed with ribbons.

ORDER OF WORKING

Bodice:

Trace the pattern on page 75 and position on the front bodice piece of the paper pattern. Mark the position of the pintucks on the fabric. Transfer the design for the flower spray (see page 74) to the centre panel.

Make the pintucks and press them flat towards the sides of the garment. Sew a length of lace to the garment so that the straight edge is covered by the pintuck. (Do not sew the lace to the pintuck.)

Using two strands of embroidery cotton, work the embroidery. Make a line of feather stitching and one of French knots on the unlaced side of each tuck. Finally, work the embroidery for the centre panel, using stem stitch for the stem, lazy daisy stitch for the flower petals and leaves, and a few French knots to complete the design.

Sleeves:

Work the sleeves to match the bodice. These have a pair of pin-tucks, with lace sewn to the garment on the outside edge of each. There is a central, double row of feather stitching with a line of French knots between them.

When the garment is completed, sew matching lace around the neck and sleeves. Trim with a narrow ribbon bow at the neck and another bow on each of the sleeves.

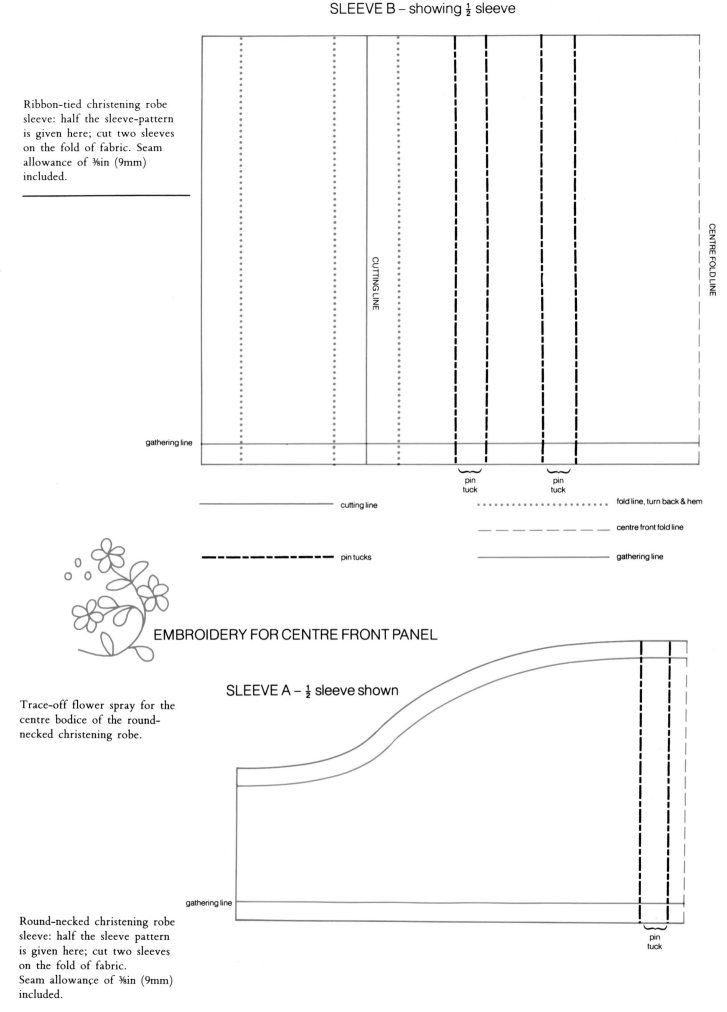

SLEEVE B – showing ½ sleeve

CUTTING LINE

CENTRE FOLD LINE

Ribbon-tied christening robe sleeve: half the sleeve-pattern is given here; cut two sleeves on the fold of fabric. Seam allowance of ⅜in (9mm) included.

gathering line

pin tuck   pin tuck

—————————————— cutting line

● ● ● ● ● ● ● ● ● ● ● fold line, turn back & hem

▬ ▬ ▬ ▬ ▬ ▬ ▬ pin tucks

– — – — – — – centre front fold line

—————————————— gathering line

EMBROIDERY FOR CENTRE FRONT PANEL

Trace-off flower spray for the centre bodice of the round-necked christening robe.

SLEEVE A – ½ sleeve shown

gathering line

pin tuck

Round-necked christening robe sleeve: half the sleeve pattern is given here; cut two sleeves on the fold of fabric.
Seam allowance of ⅜in (9mm) included.

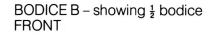

BODICE B – showing ½ bodice
FRONT

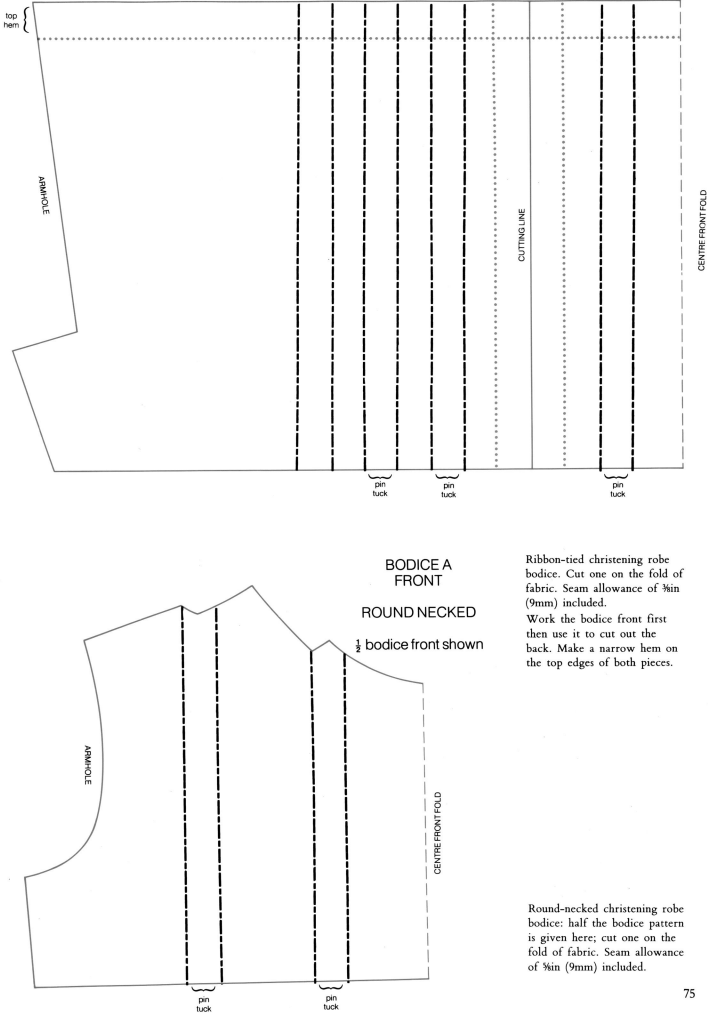

top hem

ARMHOLE

pin tuck

pin tuck

CUTTING LINE

pin tuck

CENTRE FRONT FOLD

BODICE A
FRONT

ROUND NECKED

½ bodice front shown

ARMHOLE

CENTRE FRONT FOLD

pin tuck

pin tuck

Ribbon-tied christening robe bodice. Cut one on the fold of fabric. Seam allowance of ⅜in (9mm) included.

Work the bodice front first then use it to cut out the back. Make a narrow hem on the top edges of both pieces.

Round-necked christening robe bodice: half the bodice pattern is given here; cut one on the fold of fabric. Seam allowance of ⅜in (9mm) included.

75

M O U N T -
M E L L I C K
C U S H I O N

Mountmellick embroidery could almost be described as a coarser form of Ayrshire work. It originated in Ireland in the town of Mountmellick in the 1820s and remained in fashion until the 1880s. It was executed in knitting cotton on thick, white cotton fabric with a satin face and was used for quilts, nightdress cases, sachets, brush and comb bags, dressing table mats and pillow cases.

Designs were taken from nature and included oak leaves, acorns, blackberries and blossom, vine leaves, grapes and a variety of garden flowers. The stitches were predominantly satin stitch and French knots with additional line stitches such as chain, stem, cable, feather, herringbone, coral and buttonhole stitch. The work was usually edged with buttonhole stitch and finished with a hand-knitted fringe.

This small cushion has been worked in traditional stitches and motifs, using soft embroidery cotton on a shiny satin fabric to give a contrast in textures.

By the 1880s, patterns for Mountmellick work were appearing in magazines and, as ladies found the embroidery comparatively easy, it is difficult nowadays to tell their work from that of the professional embroiderers.

Size
11in (27.5cm) diameter

MATERIALS

14in (40cm) square of white satin fabric
DMC soft embroidery cotton (Retors mat) – white – 1 skein
Embroidery crewel needle
Embroidery frame (optional)

ORDER OF STITCHING

Trace the design and transfer it to the fabric. Work the embroidery in a single thread of soft embroidery cotton. Embroider the two black-berry sprays. The blackberries and flower centres are worked in French knots with the tiny black-berry leaves in lazy daisy stitch. The flower petals are padded satin stitch. The thick stem and one side of each leaf on the smaller spray are unpadded satin stitch worked on the slant. The other side of these leaves is coral stitch and the leaves on the larger spray are outlined in cable chain stitch and have feather stitch veins. The stem on the smaller leaf spray is in herringbone stitch and the thin stems are stem stitch. Work the border around the design in buttonhole stitch, varying the length of stitches to create a 'toothed' effect on the inside edge.

Make up the work into a cushion and then knit a fringe to go all around the edge (see page 111).

The young widow in this picture by Richard Redgrave (*Throwing off her Weeds*) appears to be considering the options of the ornate pink dress and a beautiful embroidered scarf.

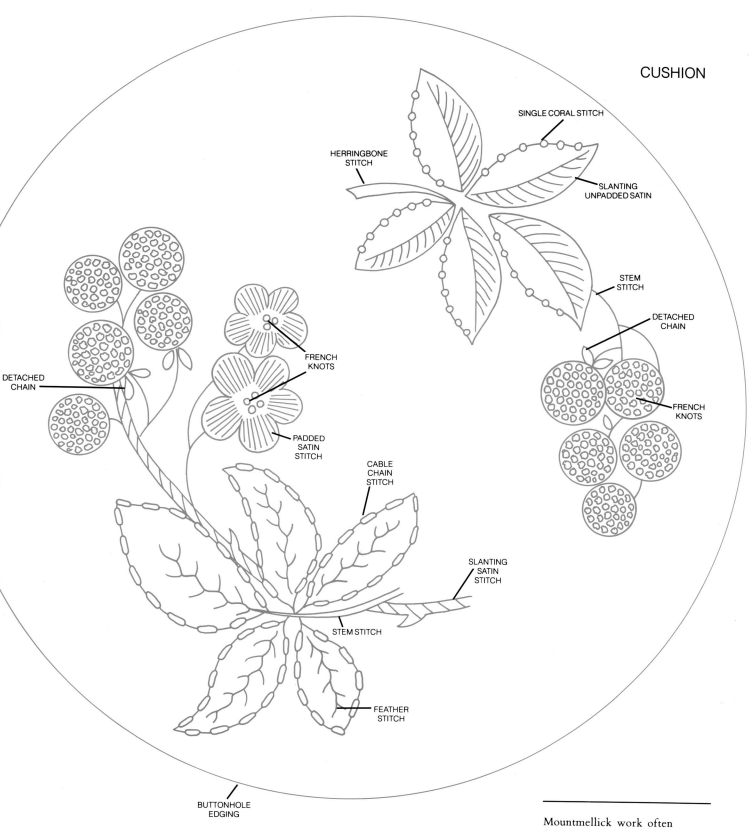

CUSHION

SINGLE CORAL STITCH

HERRINGBONE
STITCH

SLANTING
UNPADDED SATIN

STEM
STITCH

DETACHED
CHAIN

DETACHED
CHAIN

FRENCH
KNOTS

FRENCH
KNOTS

PADDED
SATIN
STITCH

CABLE
CHAIN
STITCH

SLANTING
SATIN
STITCH

STEM STITCH

FEATHER
STITCH

BUTTONHOLE
EDGING

Mountmellick work often
featured plant life in designs
and blackberry sprays (above)
are typical of early patterns.
These sprays would be ideal
for working on a cotton bed
quilt or on pillow cases.

A L P H A B E T
F O R
L I N E N S

For purely utilitarian purposes, Victorian ladies marked household linens with Indian ink or, sometimes, with cross stitch letters. However, personal possessions were often marked in a much more decorative way with imposing initial letters or monograms.

A variety of different styles of alphabet was available to the embroiderer from quite simple scrolling letters to elaborate Gothic ones or imitation strapwork. Many were additionally decorated with flowers and might also be topped by a coronet. In the latter case, it was important not to get the style appropriate for a viscount mixed up with that intended for a baron!

Such 'useful' work as embellishing sheets, towels, pillowcases and so on with initials or monograms was considered appropriate for the lady of the house, and a young bride was expected to decorate the household linen for her trousseau in this way.

The alphabet on pages 82–83 is a quite straightforward one which can be used as single initials or for monograms. Work the letters in padded satin stitch over a very close filling of long running stitches to give a pronounced raised line.

This original piece of Victorian embroidery is typical of many pretty alphabets that even today can sometimes be found in 19th-century needlework books.

MATERIALS

Cotton sheets, pillowcases etc on which to work
Stranded embroidery cotton in the same colour
Fine embroidery crewel needle
Embroidery frame

ORDER OF WORKING

Trace the appropriate letter or letters and transfer to the fabric.

Positioning individual letters –either a single initial or two or three in a spaced row – presents few problems. Remember that on sheets, the initial or monogram should be the right way up when the sheet is turned back over the blankets. (That is, wrong way up to the person in the bed.)

When making a monogram of linked, or overlapping initials, however, you will need to plan more carefully.

The modern alphabet given here is ideal for house linens or clothing and could be embellished with tiny flowers and leaf tendrils for a pretty look.

82

Trace each letter on to a separate piece of tracing paper and try different arrangements until you find one that pleases you. Then decide how the letters should interlace (ie., which lines go over which, and where sections should be removed altogether). With the monogram pictured on page 81, part of the final downstroke of the M has been omitted as has the final curl.

Make a tracing of the final arrangement and transfer it to the fabric.

Work the letters in padded satin stitch. Use four strands of stranded embroidery cotton for the filling and two strands for the satin stitch. Work sufficient long running stitches to fill the shape. You will need several rows of these filling stitches on the 'fat' areas of the letter and a single row for the 'thin' ones. Cover with very closely worked satin stitches.

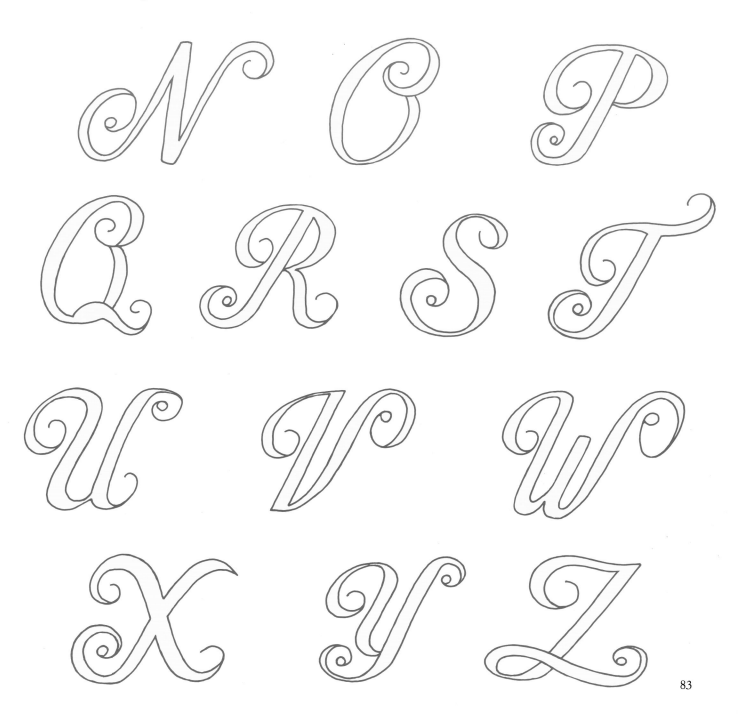

RIBBONWORK

Ribbons were used in a variety of different ways in Victorian embroidery. Sometimes they were woven in and out of a non-fraying fabric (such as canvas or leather) to make a bag or a case to hold small pieces of work. Very narrow ribbons were used instead of threads for canvaswork. Lustrous silk ribbons were used (sometimes with conventional threads) to create embroidered pictures.

Although modern polyester satin ribbons are not as soft and flexible as silk, they neither fade nor rot and are more likely to last than Victorian ribbon embroideries.

F L O W E R   P I C T U R E

Victorian ladies frequently incorporated narrow, silk, shaded ribbons into their embroidery. This gave their work an attractive three-dimensional effect and subtle changes of colour.

Ribbons were sometimes made up into flower shapes, such as rosebuds, and stitched in to the work. They were also used in the same way as conventional embroidery threads. Occasionally, ribbons were folded and caught down on the folds with tiny stitches. Stitches used with ribbons were simple-straight stitch, lazy daisy stitch, French knots and bullion knots.

Modern synthetic ribbons are not as easy to use as silk ribbons but they do come in a wonderful range of colours. Use them in conjunction with embroidery in stranded cotton or silk for the best results. The contrast between the raised areas of ribbon and the flatter thread stitches gives both depth and interest to a piece.

Choose strong fabric to work on, such as silk satin, taffeta, furnishing sateen or curtain lining. You need a fabric which will not be damaged by jerking the ribbon through it. Use a large-sized needle that will make a large hole and so avoid too much pulling.

Size

Design fits an oval 7 × 5in (18 × 13cm)

When this ribbon picture was made, the colours were the bright ones of fresh flowers. Now they have faded to the soft yellows and browns of dried ones.

MATERIALS

Cream fabric for the background
Offray polyester satin ribbons, 1⅛yd (1m) each of the following colours:
buttercup yellow ⅛in (3mm) wide
yellow gold ¹⁄₁₆in (1.5mm) wide
willow ¹⁄₁₆in (1.5mm)-wide
DMC stranded embroidery cotton, 1 skein each of the following colours:
yellow (727)
gold (743)
light green (3348)

Large-sized embroidery crewel needle (for ribbon)
Fine embroidery crewel needle (for stranded cotton)

ORDER OF WORKING

Trace the design and transfer it to the fabric. (It is really only necessary to draw in the position of the stems as a guide for the rest of the embroidery.)

Work the thread embroidery first. Use two strands of stranded cotton throughout, except for the small leaves near the top of the stems where a single strand is used. The stems are worked in stem stitch and the leaves and some flowers in lazy daisy stitch. Flower centres, some complete flowers and the 'lupins' at the top are worked in French knots. The hanging flowers are worked in bullion knots.

Next, work the ribbon embroidery. The leaves and star-shaped flower near the centre of the bouquet, as well as the buds running up the stems are in straight stitch. (The flower centre is a French knot in stranded cotton.)

Make four flowers using the buttercup-coloured ribbon and four in the yellow gold ribbon in the following way: cut a 2in (5cm) length of ribbon, run a gathering thread along the centre, pull up to make a flower shape and stitch into place on the picture.

Finally, make a double bow from the two shades of yellow ribbon and stitch in place to 'tie' the bouquet (see picture on page 85).

Follow this trace-off for the Flower Picture. Use ribbon to complete the bouquet.

F L O R E N T I N E

This needlecase cover in ribbon canvaswork has been worked in a version of the Florentine pattern which has been a favourite for centuries and was so popular for Berlin woolwork.

The stitch is a straight stitch which has many names including Florentine stitch, flame stitch and Irish stitch.

The needlecase is worked in the narrowest available double-faced ribbon – $1/16$in (1.5mm) wide on 13 threads to 1in (2.5cm) single thread canvas. This mesh enables the ribbons to lie flat and still cover the canvas adequately. Alternatively, $1/8$in (3mm)-wide ribbons and 11-thread canvas could be used. Choose white canvas for pale ribbons and 'antique' colour for dark shades.

It is essential to keep the ribbons flat, at least on the right side of the work. Using double-faced satin ribbon ensures that even if it twists on the back of the work it will still look right side up on the front.

Choose closely-related shades of the same colour for a subtle effect.

For more drama, select colours from the same family but widen the difference between the shades and add a contrasting accent. Here, three orangey shades – rust, orange and peach – are accented with a rich green.

Size
3¾ × 3¼in (9.5 × 8cm)

MATERIALS

13-mesh single thread canvas (large enough piece to be held in an embroidery frame)
$1/16$in –wide (1.5mm) Offray double-faced satin ribbon in the following colours and amounts:

forest green – 9yds (8m)

rust – 5yds (4.5m)

peach – 5yds (4.4m)

torrid orange – $3^7/8$yds (3.5m)

Tapestry needle
Embroidery frame

ORDER OF WORKING

Following the chart and key, work the book cover in Florentine stitch. Work the first row alternating the length of the stitches – the first stitch over four threads, the second over three, the third over four and so on. Work subsequent rows over four threads throughout until you reach the spine of the book where the pattern is three-four-three threads over the design.

The work is finished off with a row of stitches over three - four - three threads as at the beginning.

Above: Detail of the Florentine needlecase in ribbon work.
Below: Working chart for the Florentine pattern.

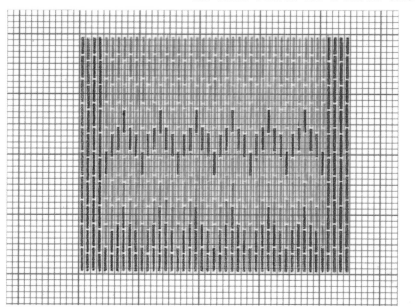

CREWELWORK

Towards the end of the nineteenth century there was a revival of interest in historical types of embroideries, particularly the crewelwork of the seventeenth century. This type of embroidery, often called Jacobean work, was originally worked in wool on a linen/cotton twill fabric. Designs owed a great deal to those found on imported Indian textiles but they also incorporated the flora and fauna of the English countryside. A central theme was the Tree of Life, laden with scrolling leaves and exotic fruit. Colourful tropical birds might fly through the branching stems and the foreground was usually composed of plants in a hummocky landscape. This would be populated with a huntsman and a variety of animals – usually all much of a size.

Stitches were usually simple ones such as stem stitch, long-and-short stitch, satin stitch, buttonhole stitch and chain stitch. Fillings included French knots, squared filling and honeycomb filling.

Nineteenth-century work followed the same themes as the earlier pieces. Crewel wools on linen or crash (a coarser linen) were the favourite materials for making window and door curtains. The latter, called *portières*, were fashionable in artistic circles – and they were also an excellent way of avoiding draughts!

This *portière*, worked in crewel wools on a beige wool twill, has all the traditional design elements. The Tree of Life grows from a landscape in which a huntsman pursues a quarry as big as himself over a hilly, flowery landscape. The leafy tree bears different sorts of blossom, including thistles and a mixture of fruit. Pomegranates exist side by side with acorns with a delightful disregard for seasonal and geographical realism. The cushion is based on just two elements of the curtain.

Detail of the door curtain (opposite). American crewelwork has a characteristic style and excellence of execution comparable to anything produced in Europe.

P O M E G R A N A T E
A N D   P A R R O T

The fabric used here is a closely-woven cotton furnishing sateen but linen or linen-look fabric, or satinized cotton (sold especially for surface embroidery), or even curtain lining could be used.

Size

16 × 16in (40 × 40cm)

MATERIALS

Cream or beige fabric 19 × 19in (48.5 × 48.5cm)
Appleton crewel wool, 1 skein each of the following colours:
gold (475, 695)
old gold (313)
beige (984, 985)
khaki (954)
brown (955, 904)
pale blue (152)
blue-green (643, 645, 646)
yellow-green (251A, 253, 254)
maroon (147)
pink (121, 142, 143)

Medium-sized crewel needle
Embroidery frame

ORDER OF STITCHING

Trace the design on pages 94–95 and transfer it to the fabric. Work the embroidery following the colours of the trace-off pattern. It does not really matter in which order you do this but it is probably easier to work the solid parts of the pattern before the areas of open filling. Use one strand of wool throughout.

Most areas are worked with long and short stitch. This includes the small flower and its leaf, the leaves and 'petals' of the pomegranate, the bird's head and some areas of its wings and tail. The bird's legs and body are in stem stitch, with the body in parallel lines curving around the shape. The long tail feather is in stem stitch and satin stitch and the smallest tail feather, individual wing feathers and beak are also in satin stitch. The pupil of the bird's eye is a French knot.

The thick stem (part of the 'tree') is made up of lines of stem stitch and the centre of the small leaf is a single line of the same stitch. The stem of the small flower and the central veins of the pomegranate leaves are in satin stitch. French knots make the centre of the small flower and outline the central section of the pomegranate. This section is filled with individual cross stitches. The outer section is filled with squared filling stitch.

Lay the lines of the trellis first, then hold in place by small stitches.

Detail of the Pomegranate and Parrot cushion (opposite). Geometric patterning with stylized plants and foliage and exotic animals and birds was a feature of crewelwork designs from the 17th century onwards.

Trace-off patterns for the cushion on page 93.
The colours used on the trace-off are keyed to the crewelwork wools listed on page 92.

SMOCKING

That eminently practical working garment, the smock, was an English idea and was very popular in the nineteenth century. Smocks were worn by carters, butchers, gardeners and other country tradesmen as well as, of course, by farmers and their workers. The master farmer's smock would usually be of a darker, more expensive fabric than the cheap unbleached cotton worn by his men.

There were two types of smocks. Round 'frocks' were the same back and front and were pulled on over the head whereas 'coat frocks' opened down the front. They were simply constructed out of a series of rectangles. The fullness was controlled across the chest and back and at the wrists by rows of special gathering, called smocking. With ordinary gathering the width of the fabric is fixed by the drawing up of the stitches. Smocking, however, gives a certain elasticity. As the wearer moves, the smocked fabric stretches with him, and then returns to its smocked width. This is a great advantage in a garment for a manual worker.

Smocks became more and more decorative with additional embroidery ornamenting the

Right: Bonnets were worn by children and adults alike to protect them from the sun while working outdoors. This one is inspired by traditional Victorian smocking.
Opposite: This round 'frock' is made with traditional motifs and techniques but in non-traditional colours.

collar, the shoulder sections and the 'boxes' on either side of the front yoke, but not the back. Patterns were basic, linear ones, such as hearts, roundels, flower shapes and zigzags, carried out in feather stitch, chain stitch and stem stitch in a variety of combinations. With this limited number of stitches the embroiderers managed to create a whole range of effects and no two smocks were ever alike.

It used to be thought that you could tell a worker's trade by the motifs chosen for the embroidery, but this seems to be a myth. There were, however, slight regional differences and the lengths of smocks varied for different callings. Shepherds would have long smocks to keep them warm on cold hillsides at night, while carters would have shorter ones, making it easier for them to get in and out of their carts.

A man would usually have two smocks, an everyday one and a more elaborately decorated one for Sundays. A bride might make an especially fine one for her husband to wear on their wedding day. Smocks were made from strong cotton or linen fabric in natural colours like beige and brown or, for wedding and Sunday smocks, cream. The cotton or linen thread used for the smocking and the embroidery would be in the same natural palette.

By the end of the century the high quality, handmade garments worn by workers were being superseded by commercially-made smocks. At the same time, however, smocking began to flourish in a new, unexpected context. It was taken up by the artistic set and was used for children's clothes and ladies' dresses. The fabrics used were, of course, finer and ladies' smocked tea gowns were often made of silk.

Smocking today is very popular for little girls' dresses and it is also an attractive way to control fullness on skirts, shirts and nightdresses for adults.

The traditional smock is still sometimes worn by Morris dancers and it can be a practical

garment for gardening, particularly if it has a pair of capacious pockets. The smock pictured is the classic round frock shape but the fabric is a grey-blue wool with contrasting white embroidery.

The smocking stitches given on page 124 are suitable for either a traditional smock or for a variety of other garments.

The embroidery motifs can likewise be used in a number of different ways, for example on a collar, a pocket or even on a box, workbag or pincushion.

FABRICS AND THREADS

A range of fabrics from silk and fine lawns to linen, calico and light-weight wools can be used for smocking. Light-weight velvet can look charming when smocked, particularly for a child's dress.

Always suit the weight and type of thread you use to the fabric. For example, Coton à Broder and no.8 Coton Perlé work well on heavier cottons and most wools. Two strands of stranded embroidery cotton or silk are a good choice for more delicate cottons, silk and for the fine wool known as nun's veiling.

This smock has less decorative embroidery than some garments of the mid-nineteenth century and may, therefore, have been for 'second-best'. The wide collar, embroidered on the edges, is a distinctive feature.

HEART MOTIFS

The pattern here is the one used for the boxes on either side of the yoke of the smock pictured on page 97. Two different weights of white cotton embroidery thread have been used (Coton à Broder no.16 and Coton Perlé no.5) to give textural interest. The hearts are worked with two lines of chain stitch (one in each thread) and an outside line of buttonhole stitch (in Coton Perlé). The small flowers in the centres are lazy daisy stitch with a French knot centre worked in Coton à Broder. The slightly larger flowers, worked in Coton

Perlé in the bottom corners, are similar but have a straight stitch in between each pair of lazy daisy stitches in Coton à Broder.

The design is enclosed with two lines of chain stitch, (one in each weight of thread), and a line of feather stitch in Coton Perlé.

The shoulders and collar are embroidered to match but with only one heart instead of two.

Above: Detail of the smock pictured on page 97.
The hearts and flowers motifs on the right are featured on the yoke of the garment and are worked in two weights of white cotton.

PINCUSHIONS

In Victorian times, pincushions were not just practical accessories for holding pins and needles, they were highly decorative objects made as Valentines and to commemorate births and weddings. A very popular form was a small, tightly-stuffed cushion on which a pattern was formed in pins or in beads speared on pins. There would be a name and possibly a sentimental message and appropriate motifs such as hearts, flowers and leaves. Additional decoration might be of lace and ribbon. The cushions would rarely have been used, since removing pins would have spoilt the pattern (as would sticking in more pins).

These little cushions are easy to make and most therapeutic to work.

MAKING PINCUSHIONS

Fillings: You need a firm base to work on and to hold the pins securely. Bran and sawdust are a good choice, but they must be thoroughly dry before you use them. Emery powder and iron filings were frequently used in the past on the basis that they would keep the pins sharp. In fact, these fillings are inclined to rust the pins. You could also choose a soft filling such as natural animal wool or used knitting wool. Synthetic fillings are also a possibility, although it can be difficult to pack them into the cushion tightly enough.

FABRICS

Always make an undercover of a closely-woven fabric such as calico or plain white cotton to hold the filling.

Top covers can be of almost anything you like. Velvet is pleasant and easy to work on,

and it has the advantage that, if you change your mind about the placing of a pin, the mark will not show (provided you remove the pin quickly). It is also a practical choice if you want to be able to use the cushion.

Pale-coloured silk or satin are lovely for layette or wedding pincushions. However, pin marks will show on these fabrics so you cannot change your mind halfway through a design.

You might like to use a lacy fabric over a coloured one, picking out part of the lace design in beads.

SHAPES

Pincushions can be round, square, rectangular – or what you will but, in general, the simple shapes are best. If you want a particularly smooth covering, the boxed cushion shape works well. Whatever shape you choose, make sure it is deep enough to take the length of the pins.

PINS AND BEADS

Choose good-quality, fine dressmaking pins in a standard length. For delicate fabrics use fine 'wedding and lace pins'.

The beads used on all the cushions shown here are readily available in craft and needlework shops. They are mostly small and inexpensive and are sold in a wide range of colours. The beads are threaded in ones or twos on to a pin and then the pin is stabbed straight into the cushion.

These velvet cushions are intended to be used as 'working' pincushions and the designs are, therefore, simple.
The silk cushions are intended as gifts and are more elaborate and delicate in execution.

A COLLECTION OF PINCUSHIONS

LILY-OF-THE-VALLEY CUSHION

Size
3 × 1¾in (7.5 × 4.5cm)
MATERIALS (for decoration)
Fine dressmaking pins
Small beads in gold, pink and green
Flower motif in lace
Beads of different sizes (to complement the type of lace flower)
Narrow lace edging

ORDER OF WORKING

The design on this small cushion is a simple one. Cover the seam round the edge with lace held in place by a row of beaded pins. Decorate the top with a lace flower motif. On the cushion shown here a whole lily-of-the-valley motif was used, plus the leaves cut from a similar motif.

Hold the flower area of the motif in place with beads of appropriate sizes and colour. Here, white beads graduate in size from the largest to the smallest blooms. Highlight the leaves with little green beads. Decorate the area between the lace edging and the flowers with a simple trellis pattern of beads.

LOVE BIRD CUSHION

The design on this larger velvet cushion was dictated by the lovebird lace motif on the top. What makes this piece particularly attractive is that the wings are left free, giving a three-dimensional effect.

The second important element was the choice of a furnishing braid to cover the edges. The braid gives the cushion a tailored look and gives scope for some large glittery beads which follow the scallops of the braid.

Size
3¼ × 3¼in (8 × 8cm)
MATERIALS (for decoration)
Fine dressmaking pins
Small beads in pink, gold, green and blue
Faceted glittery beads with one flat side
Lace motif
Furnishing braid, ½in (1cm)-wide

ORDER OF WORKING

Attach the braid around the edge of the cushion with glittery beads. The beads should follow the design, in this case a corded line making a double scallop. Position the bird motif and attach with pins to highlight the shapes. This motif shows a pair of lovebirds, so one has been highlighted with pink beads and the other with blue. Use a gold bead and a faceted bead for each. Highlight the leaves with green beads.

CHRISTENING CUSHION

This white silk-covered cushion is edged with palest pink lace and decorated largely with small pink pearl beads. The lace is wide with scallops on one side and zigzags on the other, and this has been made into a feature of the cushion. The lace is put on flat and is caught on the inner and outer angles of the

Using motifs of lace is a simple way of decorating a pincushion and a wide variety of motifs is available for every kind of scheme. Secure motifs with beads in relevant colours.

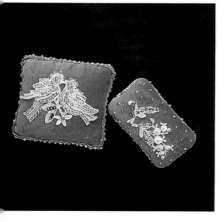

zigzag. To turn the corner, three points have been caught together.

Size

4½ × 4½in (11 × 11cm)
MATERIALS (for decoration)
Lace pins
Small pastel coloured pearl beads
Large, cup-shaped parly sequins
Wide lace trimming in the same colour
Silver pencil (or tracing paper and pencil)

ORDER OF WORKING

Attach the lace to the edge of the cushion, spacing the beads evenly around the edge of the lace.

Write the name of the child on the silk with the silver pencil and outline with beads. Alternatively, write the name in pencil on tissue paper and put in a pin on a bead at the beginning and end of the name to hold the paper in place. Then fill in the rest of the outline with beads and finally tear away the paper.

Finish off the design with bead and sequin flowers.

WEDDING CUSHION

This quite small cushion is made special by a large heart motif totally made up of pearl beads, and by the use of lace and ribbon.

Size

4 × 4in (10 × 10cm)
MATERIALS for decoration)

Lace pins
Pearl beads, ¼in (4mm) diameter
Pearl beads, ⅛in (3mm) diameter
Ready-frilled non-fray lace
Offray blue feather-edge ribbon, ½in (1cm) wide
Silver pencil

ORDER OF WORKING

Fix the lace around the edge of the cushion with a few undecorated pins. Begin and end at the centre of the bottom edge, curving the ends of the lace with scissors.

Using ⅛in (3mm) beads, pin the ribbon in place to cover the bound edge of the lace. Start and finish the ribbon at the centre of the lace pleat. Fold a separate length of ribbon into a bow and fix it in place over the join with a pin and a ¼in (4mm) bead.

Draw a simple heart shape centrally on the cushion top. Outline and fill with ¼in (4mm) beads.

A christening pincushion is a novel and attractive way of commemorating a birth. You might incorporate the child's initials in the design. Similarly, they can be given as wedding or anniversary gifts.

A VICTORIAN CHRISTMAS

The idea of the legendary Victorian Christmas conjures up a picture of snow falling steadily outside a warmly lit, comfortable room. Round the fire, all the family – grandparents, parents, aunts, uncles and, most of all, children – are gathered. There are crackers and party games, music and dancing and, of course, the whole scene is dominated by a magnificent fir tree, lit by dozens of candles and laden with decorations, sweetmeats and toys.

It was Prince Albert, the Queen's Consort, who brought this charming custom to England with him from Germany, and it has become an essential element of a traditional Christmas.

Trimming the tree is a ritual in which everyone likes to have a share, and handmade ornaments give a highly personal touch, especially when children and adults make them together.

The houses and Christmas stocking ornaments shown here are made from plastic canvas and scraps of ordinary double knitting yarn, which is much cheaper than using tapestry wool. You can work the decorations in either tent or half cross stitch, but tent stitch covers the canvas better. The jewelled ornaments are made from stuffed felt and decorated with beads.

Victorians loved ornate greeting cards and Christmas themes in particular. The tradition of sending cards at Christmas may have begun with the Victorians.

Opposite: The lighted Christmas tree, adorned with handmade ornaments, sums up the spirit of the traditional Victorian Christmas.

VILLAGE HOUSE

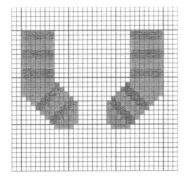

Chart for the Christmas Stocking motif. Only two colours, red and green, are used to work this design.

Size

2½ × 2¼in (6.5 × 5.5cm)

MATERIALS

Sheet of 8-mesh plastic canvas 18 × 12in (45 × 30cm), (this makes 12 houses)
Double knitting yarn in red, green and white
Tapestry needle
Black (or 'invisible') sewing thread for hanging the ornaments

ORDER OF STITCHING

Cut two pieces of plastic canvas 16 threads wide and 17 threads deep. Following the chart and key, work the house front in tent stitch with the stitches slanting from left to right. Note that two threads of the canvas are left unworked on the short wall of the house and one thread is left unworked along the bottom and chimney wall of the house. Outline the window in green back stitches and make a French-knot doorknob in red.

The back of the house is a mirror image of the front. Work the tent stitch with stitches slanting from right to left. Outline the window and make the doorknob as you did for the front.

Cut away the canvas around the chimney and roof, allowing two threads of canvas around the roof and one thread around the remaining edges for oversewing the two pieces together.

Place the back and front together and, using red yarn singly, oversew together down the short wall, along the bottom and up the chimney wall. Oversew the roof and remaining areas of the chimney with white yarn used double, taking the yarn over one or two threads of canvas as appropriate.

A CHRISTMAS STOCKING

This is worked in a similar way to the house, but only two colours are used. Make some with a green heel and toe and some with red.

Size

3¼ × 2in (8.5 × 5cm)

MATERIALS

Sheet of 8-mesh plastic canvas, 18 × 12in (45 × 30cm), (this makes 17 stockings)
Double knitting yarn, red and green

Tapestry needle
Black (or 'invisible') sewing thread for hanging the ornaments

ORDER OF STITCHING

Cut a piece of canvas 14 threads wide and 23 threads deep. Following the chart and colours indicated, work the front of the stocking in tent stitch, slanting the stitches from left to right.

The back of the stocking is a mirror image of the front. Work it in the same way but reverse the direction of the stitches.

Chart for the Village House motif. Follow the colours as shown on the chart for embroidery.

Cut away the canvas around the stocking, leaving an unworked thread of canvas all round the edge for oversewing the two sides to- gether. Place the back and front together and oversew the edges in the same colour as the toe and heel, using yarn doubled.

JEWELLED ORNAMENTS

These felt shapes decorated with beads will catch the light and sparkle in response to any slight movement or current of air. Children will enjoy helping to make them and inventing patterns.

It is important not to make the decorations so heavy that they weigh down the branches of the tree. There are several ways in which you can avoid this. Keep the decorations fairly small and use a light terylene wadding to fill them. Do not overfill the shapes but use just enough padding to make them firm and smooth. Above all, do not use too many large, heavy beads. Use just one or two for making eye-catching highlights on a decoration.

Size
Ornaments are approximately 2½in (6.5cm) across

MATERIALS

Scraps of felt
Matching sewing threads
Terylene wadding
A mixture of beads
Beading needle

ORDER OF STITCHING

From the felt, cut out pairs of simple shapes–circles, hearts, ovals approximately 3in (7.5cm) across.

Sew a pair of shapes together with back stitch approximately ⅕in

(5mm) from the edge, leaving a 1in (2.5cm) gap for turning through. Turn the shape through, and fill it with wadding. Sew up the gap.

Sew on the bead decorations in whatever pattern you choose. Simple designs, such as rows of beads following the outline of the shape work very well. Alternatively, you might like to mark out a star on a circle and outline this with beads. Another idea would be to cover the whole shape completely with tiny beads to make a really magnificent 'jewelled' piece.

Bead decorations are sewn on to the felt shapes so that they sparkle in the Christmas lights.

FINISHING TOUCHES

Many pieces of Victorian embroidery were finished with a fringe or perhaps a tassel – or even a row of tassels.

Every Victorian young lady could knot a fringe and there were innumerable methods of doing this. You could simply pull out the weft (horizontal) threads at the ends of a piece of work and then knot groups of warp (vertical) threads together. Some applied fringes were knotted and twisted into complex patterns. Fringes could also be knitted and these were often used to complete a piece of Mountmellick embroidery.

Tassels, too, varied in complexity and were added to a whole variety of embroidered articles from bags, caps and parasols to footstools, valances and antimacassars. Tassels were sometimes incorporated into a fringe or even made an entire fringe.

This firescreen is made of English coach lace and was displayed at the Great Exhibition of 1851.

Opposite: One of the first things a young girl made was a pretty, embroidered case for her needles and a treasured gift from her mother, or an aunt, was a pair of special scissors.

F R I N G E S   A N D
T A S S E L S

FRINGES

The patterns in this chapter are all for applied fringes which can be made in cotton, silk or wool to suit the embroidery. The fringe itself can be of almost any length you wish but it should balance with the depth of the knotted area.

Always suit the weight, colour and texture of a fringe to the article to which it is attached.

SIMPLE FRINGE

The number of threads used for each loop of this type of fringe depends on the weight of the fabric and the thickness of the threads. On a fine wool shawl each loop of its fringe might consist of one doubled thread of twisted crochet cotton. On a fine silk item a greater number of finer threads would be a good choice. When choosing a yarn and deciding on the number of threads, remember that the number of threads (and thus the thickness) is doubled when taken through the fabric to make the loop.

MAKING THE FRINGE

Mark out the spacing for the fringe along the edge of the fabric. Cut lengths of thread twice the finished length of fringe, plus about 2in (5cm).

Fold the strand, or strands, for the first loop in half and thread all the ends through a large needle. Take the needle through the fabric from the wrong side. Thread the needle through the loop. Tighten the loop.

Alternatively, if the fabric is suitable, you can use a fine crochet hook instead of a needle to make the fringe.

KNOTTED FRINGE

The knotted area can be as shallow or as deep as you like and the distance between the knots making up the lattice pattern is also up to you. The depth of knotted area should balance that left unknotted (ie., the latter should always be greater).

Knotting reduces the length of a fringe (eg., a single knot in six strands of crochet cotton reduces the length by over ½in (1cm). The more rows of knots you make, the shorter the finished fringe.

It is essential to keep the knotted pattern even, so it is advisable to weight the fabric – put a heavy object on it – to keep it flat. Alternatively, pin the work on to a piece of fibreboard.

A knotted fringe worked on the ends of a georgette stole or scarf.

Constructing the Knotted Fringe.

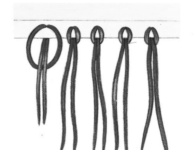

MAKING THE FRINGE

Mark out the spacing for the bunches of threads on the fabric. Cut the strands to twice the required length. Take a bunch of strands and thread one end of each through the eye of a large needle. Take the needle through the fabric and pull strands through until the ends are level.

Knot the threads together as close to the fabric edge as possible. Repeat all along the edge of the fabric.

Divide the first and second bunches of strands into two equal parts. Knot the left hand group of the first bunch with the right hand group of the second.

Repeat all the way along the work.

Make a knot in the loose strands (half bunches) at each end of the fringe to correspond.

Take the first group of strands and half the second bunch and knot together. Continue across the work in the same way.

Make as many rows of knots as desired, remembering that on the 1st, 3rd, 5th row and so on, you make a matching knot in just half a bunch of strands.

Note: On a closely-woven fabric it may be necessary to make the holes to take the fringe with a tapestry needle or knitting needle first (depending on the thickness of the fringe).

KNITTED FRINGE

This pattern gives the classic fringe for edging Mountmellick embroidery and the amount of yarn is sufficient to edge the round cushion on page 76.

It could, however, be used for a

Detail of the Knitted Fringe.

variety of purposes simply by changing the type of yarn or the colour. Worked in a coloured wool, for example, it would be ideal for a Berlin woolwork cushion. Knitted in a silky yarn, the fringe might border a heavy tablecover.

Size

2¾in (7cm) deep

MATERIALS

100 grm ball Annie Cole soft knitting cotton
Pair no.11 knitting needles

ORDER OF WORKING

Divide the ball of knitting cotton into three separate balls. Working with the three strands of yarn together, cast on 8 stitches.
Row 1: (Wind wool round needle to make 1 stitch, knit 2 together) repeat to end of row.
Repeat this row until work is long enough to go round the article.
Cast off 5 stitches.
Slip the remaining 3 stitches off the needle and unravel them all the way along the fringe.

Note: This yarn is a creamy white but will wash pure white. If the fringe is washed and dried before unravelling, it will be more crinkly. Washed after unravelling, the fringe will be straight.

A variety of tassels: from left to right, Long thin tassel, simple tassel made over a covered ring on a twisted cord, Stitched-head tassel, Large fat tassel and Shiny-headed tassel (in the foreground).

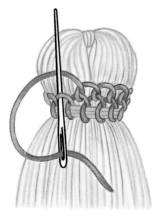

The Stitched-head tassel.

TASSELS

Five different tassels are shown in the picture ranging from a simple, long tassel with a tiny 'head' (top) and an extended, thin 'neck' (bound area) to a fat tassel with a large head and short neck. None of them is difficult to make.

LONG THIN TASSEL

This is the most basic type of tassel and can be made with any kind of thread. The one pictured is made of a mixture of ⅛in (3mm)-wide ribbon and Coton Perlé.

To make the tassel

Cut a piece of strong card about 2in (5cm) wide and slightly deeper than the required length of tassel. Wind a mixture of thread and ribbon around the card. Tie threads and ribbons tightly together at one edge and slip off the card.

If a ribbon loop is required, add this now, stitching the ends together and hiding them inside the tassel.

Using Coton Perlé, bind round the tassel starting close to the top and continuing down the tassel to the required depth–in this case approximately ¾in (2cm). Fasten off thread ends securely with a few small stitches, then run the thread up inside the neck of the tassel. Cut and trim the ends.

RING TASSEL

Work buttonhole stitch closely around a plastic or metal curtain ring. Cut a bunch of threads. Thread them through the ring and bind in place as for the long, thin tassel.

Make a twisted cord or finger chain to hang it if desired (see opposite page).

SHINY-HEADED TASSEL

This tassel has its head covered with shiny Coton Perlé to contrast with a matt skirt' of tapestry wool. The basis for the head is a wooden macramé bead which has a large central hole to take the yarn easily.

To make the tassel

Cover the bead smoothly with Coton Perlé, winding the thread over the bead and taking it through the central hole as many times as necessary. Cut a piece of stiff card, tie threads together wind wool round it as for the long, thin tassel. (Do not make the tassel too thick as it is to be pulled up inside the bead.) Fix a loop on to the top of the tassel. Thread this through the hole in the bead from bottom to top, pull it up so that the top of tassel is inside the bead. Fix in place with a few small stitches.

If the tassel skirt is too thin, enlarge it by looping extra lengths of wool on to a strong thread of the same shade. Wrap it around the existing skirt and stitch firmly in place. Cut and trim the ends.

STITCHED-HEAD TASSEL

This tassel was made entirely from Coton Perle but works equally well with wool and other yarns.

To make the tassel

Cut a piece of stiff card and wind the yarn around. Tie the loops tightly at one end before removing them from the card. Remove from the card and attach a cord, if used. Bind a thread round tightly two or three times about ½in (1cm) from the top and secure with a knot. Leave a long thread.

Work a row of buttonhole stitch into this head band. Continue working round and round the head with buttonhole stitches, working into the row below each time, but not through the tassel head, until the top is reached. Run the thread through the top row of loops, pull tightly and secure with two or three small stitches. Alternatively, work the final two or three rounds of buttonhole stitch into alternate stitches of the row below to shape it inwards. 'Lose' the remaining end of thread in the tassel. Cut and trim the ends.

Note: It may be necessary to push a little padding – cotton wool, kapok or terylene wadding – into the centre of the head as you work to make a good, rounded shape.

LARGE FAT TASSEL

This tassel is made from matt, shiny and glittery yarns in shades of turquoise with a few salmon pink threads to give highlights. The head is made from a tightly stuffed ball of stretchy stockinet fabric.

Cut a circle of fabric about 3½in (9cm) diameter. Attach a ribbon loop to the centre on the right side. Run a gathering thread around, about ½in (1cm) from the edge. Draw up and stuff very tightly before fastening off to make a smooth, round shape. Stab-stitch through from side to side on the gathering line to make the neck really firm.

Thread a needle with toning thread and bind the head to make a quilted effect. Take the needle through the neck each time. Cut a piece of thick card 6in (15cm) wide by 3in (7.5cm) deep. Using an assortment of threads, take 6-8 ends together and wind them around the card a few times, working along it.

Thread a tapestry needle with a double length of strong cotton. Knot the ends together and take the

needle under the first bunch of 6 - 8 threads on the edge of the card and through the loop made by the knot in the cotton. Pull tight. Take the needle under the bunch once more, making a coral knot. Make another knot by taking the needle under the lefthand loop of the coral knot.

Continue wrapping the thread round the card and making knots round bundles of 6-8 threads until the fringe is long enough to fit tightly around the neck of the tassel. Keep each knotted bunch as close to the previous one as possible.

Using double sewing cotton, stitch the skirt round the neck. Finish by binding several times around the neck. Use the same shade and type of thread as that used to 'quilt' the head.

Note: Instead of quilting the head and topping with a ribbon loop, it could be covered with buttonhole stitch. Add a cord to finish.

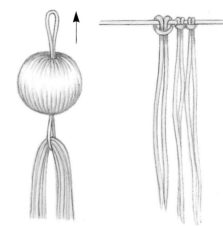

Shiny-headed tassel with large macramé bead.

TWISTED CORD

You will need a friend to help you with this project.

Take a length of yarn six times the required length of the finished cord. Fold the yarn in half and knot the ends. Each of you puts a pencil in the end loops. With the thread stretched, you twist the pencils clockwise until the threads are tightly wound together. Without relaxing the tensioned threads, fold the cord in half and twist the other way. Pull very tightly before releasing. A thicker cord can be made by using two (or three) loops of thread.

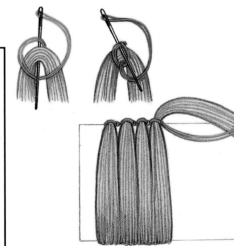

Making the Large Fat Tassel.

TECHNIQUES
FOR PERFECTION

Embroidery is a delightful and relaxing hobby which needs very little basic equipment. Needles, scissors and perhaps some sort of frame are all you need to get started. In most cases, you can carry a project around with you and work on it wherever you go.

Embroidery is not difficult and all the projects in this book are well within the capabilities of a reasonably competent embroiderer. Even the absolute beginner should take heart. Almost anyone can master a few basic stitches with a little practice and can achieve some very pleasing results. Do not start with anything too large or with very small, fine stitchery or you might get discouraged and never embroider again.

Having chosen your project, there are some basic techniques which will be invaluable to you and these will help you to produce perfect pieces of embroidery.

Right: A workbox was an essential piece of furniture in a Victorian home. Some were handsome, standing pieces, as in this engraving. Others were simple wooden boxes, similar to those used today.

Opposite: Essential ingredients of a workbox include thread, needles, scissors and a frame.

TRANSFERRING DESIGNS

Once you have decided on a design you will need to transfer it to the fabric. There are a variety of ways to do this.

PRICK AND POUNCE

This is the traditional way of transferring a design to fabric. Trace the design on tracing paper. Then, from the wrong side, prick holes along the design lines, quite close together. Use a sharp sewing needle. (It helps if you push the needle eye into a cork.)

Pin the fabric on to a board. Place the tracing (right side up) on top. Using a cottonwool bud, rub powdered French chalk (or talcum powder) lightly over the whole pattern. The powder will go through the holes, marking the pattern lines on the fabric. On light-coloured fabrics, mix a little powdered charcoal with the French chalk to make it pale grey. Remove the paper carefully and then paint over the pounced lines with watercolour paint. Use blue for white fabric and white for darker shades.

RUNNING STITCH METHOD

Trace the design on to tissue paper. Baste the paper to the fabric at the edges. Thread a needle with ordinary sewing thread and work running stitches round the outlines of the design. Then carefully tear away the tissue paper. The design is outlined by stitched lines on the fabric. Any threads not covered by embroidery can be removed when the work is completed.

TRACING THROUGH THE FABRIC

This simple method of transferring can be used on thin, light-coloured fabrics. The design is traced on the fabric using a water-soluble pen, sold especially for embroidery. The traced line will disappear with washing, or can be sponged away by gently dabbing with a clean, damp cloth. Light-dissolvable pens are also available.

Trace the design on to tracing paper, using a black fibre-tip pen. Spread thin fabric over the tracing. Trace the design on to the fabric, using a water-soluble or light-dissolvable pen.

For slightly thicker fabrics you will need a light source behind the work to enable you to clearly see the lines of the design. Fix the tracing, with fabric on top, to a window, using masking tape. Trace the design.

FRAMES

The decision as to whether or not to work embroidery in a frame is entirely up to you. Some people almost invariably work in a frame, others prefer to work with the fabric in hand.

The advantage of a frame is that it holds the work taut while you are working and thus helps prevent the fabric from distorting. This is particularly important when working on canvas where the diagonal pull of the stitches quickly distorts the shape. The embroidery then requires extensive damping and blocking to rectify the distortion.

An embroidery frame is also useful when working surface embroidery and helps to prevent the work becoming wrinkled and pulled. With stitches which involve scooping the fabric, such as chain stitch, however, it is impossible to work them with the fabric tautly stretched in a frame. It is necessary to temporarily slacken off the fabric in the frame from time to time.

There are basically two different types of frame on the market, rectangular shapes and round ones.

RECTANGULAR FRAMES

Some rectangular frames are heavier than others. Most have rollers at the top and bottom with a strip of webbing fixed to each for attaching the work. Some have side struts with holes. Others have screws instead of straight struts for adjusting the depth. Some types of frame are mounted on a stand which leaves both hands free for working the embroidery. These are useful but they do take up a lot of space.

One readily-available type of frame consists of rollers at the top and bottom and fixed-length side struts into which the rollers slot. The rollers are held firmly in place by means of metal nuts on the side struts. These lap frames come in a range of different sizes. The critical measurement is the width (i.e. length of the webbing attached to the roller). This must be greater than the width of the piece of work. The depth (i.e. length of the struts) is less important and any excess fabric is rolled around the bottom roller. When the top section of the embroidery is completed this is then rolled around the top roller and the unworked section unrolled from the bottom.

Before mounting the embroidery in the frame, sew tape down both side edges of the fabric, using diagonal basting stitches. Turn under and baste ½in (1cm) at the top and bottom of the work to prevent stitches tearing the fabric when the frame is tightened. Then, starting at the centre, oversew the turned-in top and bottom edges, very securely, to the webbing on the rollers. Assemble the frame and take up the slack on the fabric by turning the rollers. Tighten the nuts on the struts to keep the rollers in place.

Lace the sides of the fabric to the struts using a strong button thread or fine string.

Rectangular frames are best for all but very small pieces of canvaswork. The work is held very firmly both horizontally and vertically and there is a minimum of distortion of

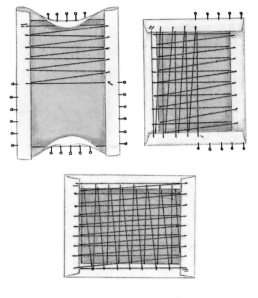

Mounting embroideries: (1) hold embroidery to the mounting board with pins pushed into the edges. Lace opposite sides together; (2) repeat with remaining opposite sides, to complete the lacing; (3) remove the pins.

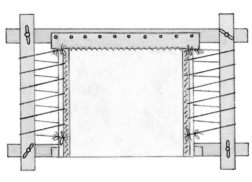

Rectangular frames: Lace the sides of the fabric to the struts using a strong button thread or fine string.

117

the canvas when stitching. These frames can be used also for other types of embroidery and are particularly useful for larger pieces.

ROUND FRAMES

The simple hand-held embroidery hoop is the most widely used type of frame. These round frames are available in a whole range of sizes from 4-12in (10-30cm) diameter. The most usual type is made of wood and consists of a continuous fixed inner ring and an outer, cut one which has a metal screw for tightening and loosening the frame.

It is advisable to bind the inner ring with bias binding before mounting your work in it to prevent the fabric slipping. This is particularly helpful if you are using slippery fabrics.

To mount the embroidery in the frame, simply lay the fabric over the inner frame. Loosen the screw on the outer one and place it over the top. Adjust the fabric in the frame until it is taut and then tighten the screw on the frame.

It is also possible to buy decorative round and oval frames which can be used both for working the embroidery and displaying the work afterwards.

DAMPING AND STRETCHING

During embroidery the work may get slightly out of shape, even if a frame is used.

CANVASWORK

This is where distortion is most likely to happen. Using a rectangular frame helps considerably towards avoiding the problem

and a light spray and press from the wrong side might well be all that is necessary.

If, however, the piece has become mis-shapen you can put things right by damping and stretching the work.

Take a piece of board larger than the work and cover with several layers of absorbent paper and then a clean cloth.

Dampen the back of the canvaswork – a spray bottle is useful for this – and lay it on the board, right side down.

Pin one edge of the work to the board with drawing pins, making sure the line is absolutely straight. Position the pins about 1-1½in (2.5-4cm) from the stitching and ½in (1cm) apart. Using a ruler and set square, make sure the work is square. Pulling and stretching the fabric as you go, pin one adjacent edge in place in the same way. Repeat with the last two sides.

Leave work pinned to the board until it has dried out naturally. This may take several days. Repeat the process if necessary.

EMBROIDERY

For surface embroidery and counted-thread embroidery, such as cross stitch, that has become distorted, drastic measures are not necessary. Any wrinkles and puckers are usually easily removed by pressing. The temperature of the iron and whether it is used over a damp cloth, with or without steam, depends very much on the fabric. It is advisable to test a scrap piece of fabric before risking spoiling a finished piece of work.

In general, place the work face down on a padded surface – this might be a folded towel with a piece of clean cotton fabric on top. Then either press carefully with a steam iron or with a dry iron and damp cloth. The padded surface prevents the stitching from becoming flattened and helps prevent the iron leaving imprints on the fabric.

MOUNTING

You might want to make a piece of embroidery into a picture or to use it as a box top. In this case you will need to mount it first.

The best way to do this is to lace it on to a piece of strong cardboard, hardboard or plywood. The method described here is for a rectangular or square piece of work but can be adapted for an oval or round one.

Cut the piece of board a fraction smaller than the size of the finished work, to accommodate the thickness of the fabric. Trim the embroidery, leaving a generous turning all round the edge. The width depends on the size of the piece of work but, in general, should be at least 1in (2.5cm).

Place the embroidery on top of the board, centring it carefully and making sure it is square. Hold in place with pins pushed into the edges of the board.

Turn the work face down. Using a strong thread and starting at the middle of a side, lace two opposite edges of the fabric tightly together. Remove the pins. Repeat with the other two sides, folding the corners. With thicker fabrics, trim away some of the fabric from the corners to make them lie flat.

Often, especially with fine fabrics, it is a good idea to pad the work slightly to give a softer texture. Simply lace a piece of plain, soft fabric over the board before fixing the embroidery in place.

Sometimes, as when making greeting cards, a solid mount is not necessary or desirable. In this case, cut a piece of thin card very slightly smaller than the finished shape. Using this as a guide, lightly mark the wrong side of the work with pencil. Trim away the fabric leaving a ½in (1cm) turning. Cut a piece of wadding, the same size as the card. Lay the embroidery face down, put the wadding and card on top. Stick the fabric turning down on to the card with fabric glue.

When working on a curved shape, you will need to snip into the curves to ensure that the fabric lies flat.

An English mid nineteenth-century Berlin woolwork sampler showing cross stitch, Hungarian stitch, Florentine and basket stitches and laid work.

119

STITCH LIBRARY

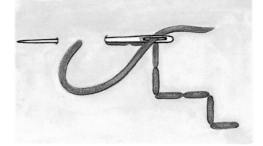

Back stitch This simple and useful stitch is used for outlining and, worked on a small scale, can follow quite intricate shapes accurately. Keep stitches even in size.

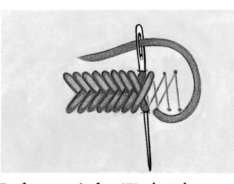

Basket stitch Work between marked parallel lines. This stitch is used either as a border or as a filling stitch.

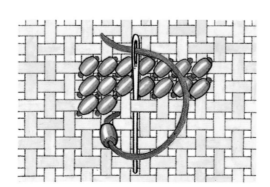

Beaded half cross stitch This is the simplest way to attach beads to canvas. Thread a bead on to each diagonal stitch, making sure that all the beads lie in the same direction.

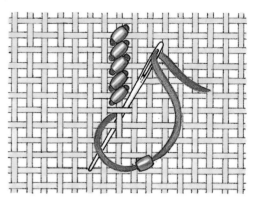

Beaded tent stitch Thread a bead on to the stitches as you work. Work vertically down the canvas. It is important that the bead size matches the canvas gauge. If beads are too large for the holes they will force the threads out of alignment and the beads will not lie neatly.

Braid stitch The band of stitching can be straight or curved. Keep the two sides of the braid parallel, and the stitches evenly neat.

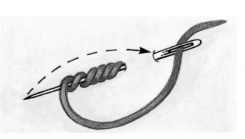

Bullion knot This is worked in a similar way to a long French knot. ·Bring the needle up through the fabric, make a backstitch the intended length of the knot. wind the thread round the needle to make the desired length of knot.

Hold the thumb on the coiled thread, pull the needle through and re-insert it where it originally went into the fabric.

Buttonhole edging First, small running stitches are worked round the shape to hold the edge, then buttonhole stitch is worked to cover the running stitches.

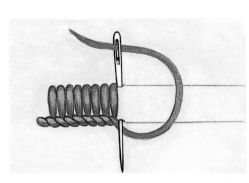

Buttonhole stitch This stitch is used extensively in cutwork and to give raw edges an attractive finish. It can be worked along curved and straight lines.

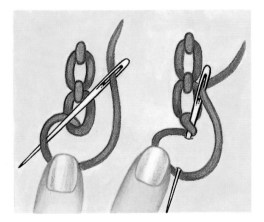

Cable chain stitch This outline stitch is similar to ordinary chain stitch but has a straight bar between each 'link' of the chain.

Chain stitch This stitch is used both for outlining and for filling a shape. The 'links' of the chain can be open and round or pulled tighter so that the 'link' chain closes.

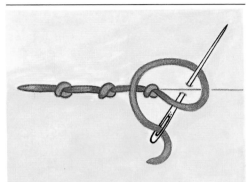

Coral stitch This outline stitch makes an attractive knotted line. Hold the thread loosely with the thumb while making the knot.

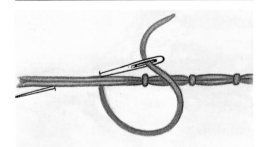

Couching This is a method of holding a thick thread, or several threads, down on the fabric surface, thus creating a raised line. Lay the thread to be couched along the design line and hold in place with the left (or non-working) hand. Tie down with a finer thread as shown. More stitches will be needed when working round a curve.

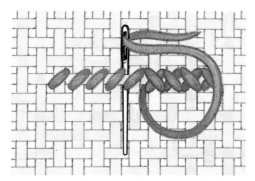

Cross stitch Modern samplers are usually worked in this stitch. It is particularly suited to evenweave fabrics. Cross stitch is worked in two stages, from right to left or left to right but the top stitch always lies in the same direction.

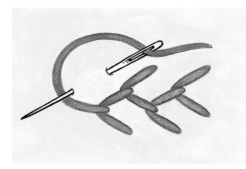

Feather stitch This stitch can be worked in straight lines or can follow a curve. In its simplest form, take one stitch to the right of the line, the next to the left and so on. Make multiple rows by working two or three stitches alternately on each side of the line.

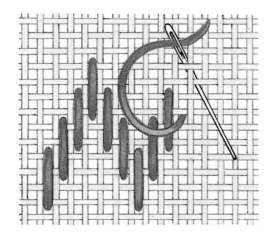

Florentine stitch This is an upright stitch usually worked over four threads, staggering stitches so that the rows form zigzag lines. The pattern is made by using several colours.

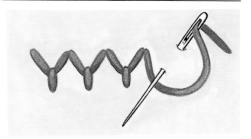

Fly stitch This stitch is worked singly in vertical or horizontal rows. Different effects can be achieved by varying the size, or the thickness of thread.

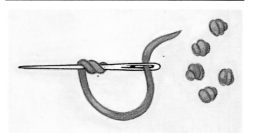

French knots This stitch is sometimes used for flower centres and can be used as a filling stitch. To work, take a small stitch and, with the needle still in the fabric, wind the thread twice round the needle. Hold the coiled thread in place as the needle is pulled through. Tighten the knot and re-insert the needle into the fabric where it first emerged.

Half cross stitch This stitch looks like tent stitch when worked but uses less yarn and does not cover the canvas as well.

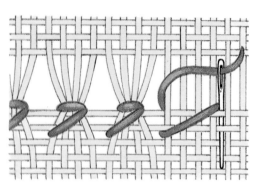

Hemstitch This is a decorative way of finishing the edges of items such as household linen and handkerchiefs. It can be worked on white linen, cotton or on delicate fabrics. Decide on the depth of hem needed plus turnings and withdraw two or three threads at this level. (To do this, snip threads in the centre of the work and withdraw the threads each side. Darn in the ends of the drawn threads and cut off the excess.) Turn up the hem to the level of the withdrawn threads and baste in place. Work hemstitches as shown.

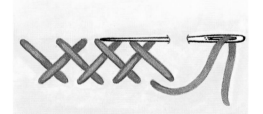

Herringbone stitch This is a border stitch and can be used as the basis for a variety of composite stitches. For the best effect, keep the spaces between the stitches even.

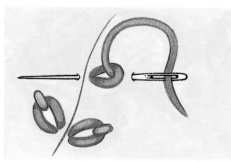

Lazy daisy (detached chain) stitch Work as for Chain stitch but hold each loop in place with a small stitch.

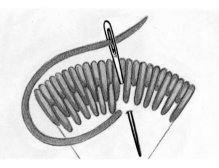

Long-and-short stitch This stitch is often used for shading. It is worked like satin stitch but the first row of stitches, outlining the shape, is worked with alternating long and short stitches. Subsequently, the stitches are all the same length.

Padded satin stitch (see also page 125) A slightly raised effect is created by first filling the shape with running, chain or stem stitches.

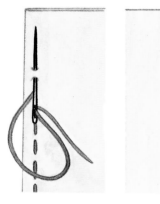

Pintucks These tiny, decorative pleats are often worked on baby clothes and lingerie. Pleats can be as narrow as you like but never wider than 3mm (⅛in). Mark the top and bottom of the pleat's fold line, fold the fabric along this line and press. Measure and mark the required width of pleat and work a line of running stitches through both layers of fabric.

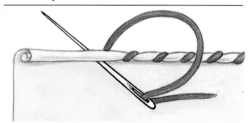

Rolled hem This is a pretty way to neaten the edge of a delicate fabric. Roll the edge gently between thumb and forefinger and, as you roll, stitch as shown.

SMOCKING STITCHES

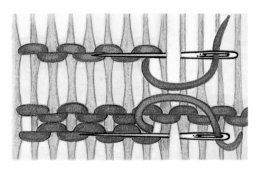

Cable stitch Not as tight a stitch as stem stitch it holds the gathers fairly firmly.

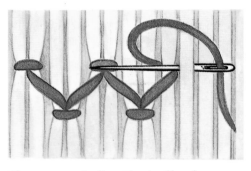

Chevron stitch Basically the same as surface honeycomb stitch but more widely spaced. The fabric is held very loosely.

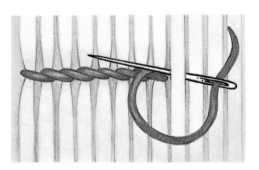

Stem stitch This stitch is very like the stem stitch used in embroidery. It is the tightest of the stitches used in smocking and several rows are often worked at the top edge of a piece of work to 'set' the pleats.

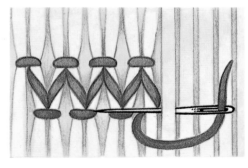

Surface honeycomb This is a loose stitch and is therefore usually worked at the bottom of a piece of smocking where fullness is needed.

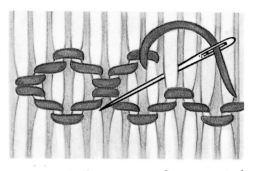

Wave stitch Rows of wave stitch can be worked with the preats aligned one below the other. Alternatively, make a diamond pattern by placing the 'crests' of one row immediately below the 'troughs' of the row above.

Satin stitch This is a useful stitch for filling shapes. When working, it is important that the shape is followed accurately to give it definition and that stitches are even and close together, completely covering the fabric. An effect of light and shade can be achieved by varying the direction of the stitch.

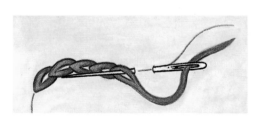

Split stitch This can be used for working stems, to outline, or it can be used as a filling. Soft twisted or floss (untwisted) thread works best for this stitch. The needle goes

through the thread, thus splitting it. Stranded thread can also be used and in this case, the needle passes between the strands.

Tent stitch This stitch can be worked in a diagonal direction or horizontally over the canvas.

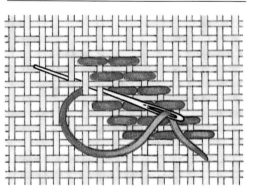

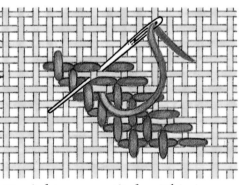

Upright cross stitch This is cross stitch worked with vertical and horizontal stitches (instead of diagonal stitches). It can be used as a filling stitch and contrasts effectively with conventional cross stitch.

INDEX

Aesthetic Movement 8
Aida fabric 20
Alphabet for linen 80
    Patterns for 82–3
Alphabet sampler 25
    Chart for 24
Anglo-Indian work 64
Arts and Crafts Movement 8
Ayrshire work 68

Back stitch 120
Basket stitch 121
Beading 10
Beading on canvas 10
Beading equipment 10–12
Beads 10–12
Beadwork designs:
    Floral Footstool 12
    Gothic Cushion 14
    Jet-beaded Dress 16
    Silken Purse 18
Beadwork stitches:
    Half-cross stitch 123
    Tent stitch 125
Berlin woolwork 8, 30
    Designs:
    Canvas lace box 38
    Chrysanthemum Cushion 34
    Slippers 32
    Golden Bee Box 38
    Turkish-style Spectacles Case 36
    Stitches: Half-cross stitch 123
    Tent stitch 125
Braid stitch 120
Buttonhole stitch 121

Cable chain stitch 121
Cable stitch 124
Canvas:
    Beading on 10
    Ribbon embroidery on 88
    Woolwork on 31
    Meshes 10, 25, 31
Chantilly Lambrequin 38
Christening Pincushion 102
Christening Robes: 70–5
    Ribbon-tied 70
    Round-necked 72
    Patterns for 74–5
Christmas, Victorian 104
Christmas Ornaments 104
    Designs:
    Jewelled Ornament 107
    Christmas Stocking 106
    Village House 106
Coral stitch 121
Couching 121

Crewel wools 92
Crewelwork 90
    Design: Pomegranate and Parrot
    Cushion 92
Cross stitch 122
Cushions:
    Chrysanthemum 30
    Pomegranate and Parrot 92

Damping and stretching canvas 118
Direct tracing 116
Dover Charity School 26

Embroidery:
    on fabric 40
    on smocks 84
    with ribbon 99
    stitches 120–5
Elizabeth Wardle's Frame 56
Embroidery frames 117
Englishwoman's Domestic Magazine 10,16
Evenweave fabrics, (Aida, Hardanger,
    Linda) 20

Feather stitch 122
Fish scales 6
Flame stitch 88
Floral Footstool 12
Floral Greetings 50
Florentine design 88
Flowers and bird motifs 26
Flower Frame 56
Flower picture (in ribbon) 86
Flower, fruit and plant designs:
    Blackberries 76–9
    Briar Rose 53
    Chrysanthemum 34
    Fruit and Flowers 60–3
    Garlands and leaves 46–9
    Lily-of-the-Valley 102
    Pansy 52
    Pomegranate and Parrot 95
Fly stitch 122
Frames 116–18
French knots 124
Fringes 108
    Designs:
    Knitted Fringe 111
    Knotted Fringe 110
    Simple Fringe 110

Georgette Stole 42
Gothic Cushion 14
Golden Bee Box 38
Greeting Cards 50

Handkerchief 54

Heart motifs 99
Hemstitch 123
Herringbone stitch 123
House and Garden Sampler 23

Indian textiles 90

Jet-beaded Dress 16
Jacobean work 90
Jet beads 16
Jewelled Ornament 107

Knitted Fringe 111
Knotted Fringes 110

Lazy Daisy stitch 123
Linen, alphabet for 82–3
Lily-of-the-Valley Pincushion 102
Love Bird Pincushion 102

Manser, Eliza 26
Morris, William (1834–1896) 8, 56
Morris, Marshall & Faulkner & Co.
    (1861) 8
Mounting embroidery 119
Mountmellick, Ireland 76
Mountmellick cushion 76, 77
Mountmellick work 76

National Female Schools in Ireland 20
Needlework in education 20
Needlecase in ribbonwork 88

Padded satin stitch 123
Paisley table cloth 64
Pearl beads 103
Pincushions 100
    Designs:
    Christening 102
    Lily-of-the-Valley 101
    Love Bird 101
    Wedding 102
    Fabrics, filling, etc. 101
    Pins, beads, etc. 101
Pintucks 68, 70, 72,
    74–5, 124
Plastic canvas 104–5
Pressing embroidery 119
Prick and pounce technique 116

Rectangular frames 117
Ribbon embroidery 86
Ribbon needlecase 88
Ribbon picture 86
Rolled hem 124
Round frames 118
Royal School of Art Needlework 8

Samplers 20–9
  Designs:
    House and Garden 23
    Alphabet 25
    Eliza Manser's 26
School of Art Needlework (*see under*
  Royal School of Art Needlework)
Silk canvas 7
Silk handkerchief 54
Slippers 33
Smocking 96
Smocking stitches 124–5
Stitches for embroidery:
  Back stitch 120
  Basket stitch 120
  Beaded half cross stitch 120
  Beaded tent stitch 120
  Braid stitch 120
  Bullion knot 120
  Buttonhole edging 121
  Buttonhole stitch 121
  Cable chain stitch 121
  Cable stitch 124
  Chain stitch 121
  Chevron stitch 124
  Coral stitch 121
  Couching 121

Cross stitch 122
Feather stitch 122
Florentine stitch 122
Fly stitch 122
French knots 122
Half cross stitch 123
Hemstitch 123
Herringbone stitch 123
Lazy daisy stitch 123
Long-and-short stitch 123
Padded satin stitch 123
Satin stitch 125
Stem stitch (smocking) 124
Split stitch 125
Upright cross stitch 125
Wave stitch 125
Surface honeycomb stitch 124

Table cloth, Paisley 64
Table runner 60
Tambouring 10
Tapestry needles 30
Tassels 110
  Designs:
    Large fat 113
    Long thin 112
    Ring 112

Shiny-headed 112
Stitched-head 112
Tracing through fabric 116
Transferring designs 116
Turkish-style Spectacles Case 36
Twisted cord 113

Upright cross stitch 125

Valance, beaded 14
Velvet cap 46
Victorian Christmas 104
Victorian fabrics 6
Victorian home life 6
Village House 106

Wardle, Elizabeth 56
Waxing thread 10
Wedding pincushion 102
Whitework 68
  Designs:
    Alphabet for linen 80
    Mountmellick cushion 76
    Ribbon-tied Christening Robe 70
    Round-necked Christening Robe 72

ACKNOWLEDGEMENTS

I wish to thank the following for their help in making this book possible: Shirley Bartlett, Felix Cope, Rosemary Ford, Ann Mary Johnstone, Mary Pilcher and Elizabeth Stephens, who kindly loaned me their precious pieces of Victorian embroidery. Pamela Atkinson for creating the beautiful christening robe bodice and sleeve designs; Ann Mary Johnstone who created the tassels; Mary Pilcher who designed both of the ribbon embroidered pictures, and the smock; and Sally Saunders who created both the canvas lace design and the round, Mountmellick cushion.

Thanks, too, to Moyra McNeill for her advice and for kindly reading the text for me and to Di Lewis for her delightful photographs. Most of all, thank you to my husband, Jack Parker, for his moral support – as always.

SUPPLIERS OF YARNS USED IN THIS BOOK

Appleton's Embroidery Wools
Appleton Bros Ltd, Lambs Yard,
Church Street, Chiswick, London
W4 2PE

Annie Cole Knitting Cotton
Annie Cole, 73 Princes Way,
Wimbledon, London SW19 6HY
(Available by mail order)

DMC Threads
Dunlicraft Ltd, Pullman Road,
Wigston, Leicester LE8 2DY

Madeira Threads
Madeira Threads (UK) Ltd, Thirsk
Industrial Park, York Road,
Thirsk, North Yorkshire YO7 3BX

Offray Ribbons
Offray Ribbons Ltd, Ashbury,
Roscrea, Co. Tipperary, Ireland